Social Entrepreneurship and Grand Challenges

Emilio Costales • Anica Zeyen

Social Entrepreneurship and Grand Challenges

Navigating Layers of Disruption from COVID-19 and Beyond

palgrave
macmillan

Emilio Costales
School of Business and Management
Royal Holloway, University of London
Egham, UK

Anica Zeyen
School of Business and Management
Royal Holloway, University of London
Egham, UK

ISBN 978-3-031-07449-3 ISBN 978-3-031-07450-9 (eBook)
https://doi.org/10.1007/978-3-031-07450-9

This Palgrave Macmillan imprint is published by the registered company Springer Nature Switzerland AG.
The registered company address is: Gewerbestrasse 11, 6330 Cham, Switzerland

Acknowledgments

We would like to extend our sincerest gratitude to Cátia Rodrigues and Nour El Gazzaz, PhD students at Royal Holloway, University of London. Without their unwavering emotional and philosophical support, this book could not have been written.

Contents

List of Figures

CHAPTER 1

Social Entrepreneurship and Grand Challenges

Abstract The COVID-19 pandemic was a once in a lifetime disruption to all aspects of life. It was a truly global experience as its impact was felt by communities across the globe. The magnitude of the impact felt in loss of lives, disruptions to work and supply chains, and to societal norms—to name but a few—highlighted how unprepared the international community was to deal with a challenge of that size. The pandemic spotlighted inefficiencies within the systems that govern society, and how ill-equipped we are to address these. COVID-19 has left an indelible mark that has drastically altered the future of economic and social life. This chapter introduces the concepts of grand challenges and wicked problems, and how social entrepreneurship may be used as a tool to meet society's grand challenges

Keywords Grand challenges • Wicked problems • Sustainable development goals

it always seems impossible until it's done
—Nelson Mandela, 2001

E. Costales, A. Zeyen, *Social Entrepreneurship and Grand Challenges*, https://doi.org/10.1007/978-3-031-07450-9_1

1.1 Grand Challenges, Wicked Problems, and the SDGs

As we seek to rebuild and move forward from the COVID-19 pandemic, we are faced with questions surrounding what we as a society can learn from this pandemic, and how we can use this to address current and future grand challenges such as poverty, climate change, and health. The pandemic highlighted the complexity and intertwined nature of global challenges as well as the fragility of the status quo. So, what is the role of business, the state, and communities in addressing these challenges? How might we efficiently move towards a world where the United Nations Sustainable Development Goals (SDGs) can become a reality? Moving closer to the answers to these questions is the underlying aim of this book.

In the context of grand challenges, social entrepreneurship and social innovation are often discussed as potential solutions or avenues towards solutions (Bacq et al., 2020; van Wijk et al., 2019). However, rather than arguing for social entrepreneurship as a silver bullet to grand challenges, our aim is to theoretically and empirically showcase how social entrepreneurship can serve as one useful tool to solve grand challenges beyond the COVID-19 pandemic—yet not on its own, but through communication with other system parts.

Grand challenges are extremely complex problems of global proportions that can potentially be solved through concerted collaborative efforts from multiple stakeholders (e.g. Ferarro et al., 2015; George et al., 2016). Such collaborative effort necessitates clear definition of problems, and arguably more importantly, clear and simple articulation of the goals to be achieved. Thus, understanding what the outcome should be is essential to guide innovation.

The concept of grand challenges can be traced back to German mathematician Dr. David Hilbert. In 1900, Dr Hilbert delivered a lecture at the International Congress of Mathematicians in Paris, with the purpose of promoting dialogue between mathematicians to further development of the field and cooperation between disparate research streams. To do so, he presented 23 problems that, together, formed the grand challenges within the mathematical sciences for the next century. Hilbert argued that drawing insight from various branches of mathematics was vital for facilitating the advancement of science beyond mathematics (see Hilbert, 1902). Over 100 years after Hilbert coined the term, the Bill and Melinda Gates Foundation and health scholars under the leadership of Dr. Abdallah

Daar applied the concept to global health. Since then, organizations such as Grand Challenges Canada have applied the concept more broadly to sustainability challenges.

In 2015, the member states of the United Nations adopted the 2030 agenda for sustainable development, with 17 Sustainable Development Goals (SDGs) aimed at creating global cooperation to tackle economic issues of poverty and growth; social issues such as health, education, and inequality; and environmental issues such as forest, soil, and ocean preservation (e.g. UNGA, 2015). Yet, with only 8 years left, it is unlikely that the global community will meet these goals by the 2030 deadline. The Secretary General of the United Nations, António Guterres, points out that uptake of the 2030 agenda has not been at the levels that it should be (UNGA, 2021). The UN further suggests that such hesitancy to fully embrace the SDGs may have left the world unprepared for the COVID-19 pandemic (UNGA, 2021).

After the Ebola crisis of 2014, Bill Gates, CEO of Microsoft and Co-founder of the Bill & Melinda Gates foundation, pointed out, in a now famous TED talk, that the world was not prepared for the next global outbreak[1]. The COVID-19 pandemic, beginning in 2020, showed the world that we were indeed not ready to the extent that we could have and should have been. Governments around the world implemented social distancing and lockdown measures to combat the virus and protect vital pieces of infrastructure, such as hospitals, from being overwhelmed. Thousands of businesses were closed, millions of people lost their jobs, and governments around the world scrambled to determine the best way to navigate this crisis. Questions began emerging in the social discourse around what the role of government should be, what role should the private sector play, what individuals and communities can do to support navigating the crisis, and the inequalities facing marginalized communities.

At the same time, the COVID-19 pandemic has shown that there is considerable capacity for community development and procedural transformation in the face of crisis, through collaborative and cooperative behavior. Society has learned that taken for granted uses of space (such as travelling into an office) need to be re-thought: work can be conducted from home with the same or better outcomes than in an office. Furthermore, certain 'workarounds' serve to include marginalized

[1]You can access Bill Gates' TED talk here: https://www.ted.com/talks/bill_gates_the_next_outbreak_we_re_not_ready?language=dz

communities. For example, disabled people can be included in ways the current work paradigm thought impossible through remote working.

The impact of this pandemic is sure to have long-term implications for the way we conduct social and economic life in the future (e.g. Kraus et al., 2020; WHO, 2020). As climate change continues its relentless march, unless we can grab hold of the reins, the possibility of similar upheaving epidemics is greater and greater (WHO, 2020). What can we learn from the impact of this pandemic and what can it teach us about the global hesitancy to fully commit to the Sustainable Development Goals? How can we reach all 17 SDGs? Prepare for the next epidemic? Grow our communities? Build our cities? Empower bottom-up sustainable growth and unite to address the grand challenges of our time?

Here, a key takeaway from Dr Hilbert's lecture was that the cause of failure when searching for a solution is often because easier problems, perhaps a cause of the initial problem, remain unsolved. The goal then, is to find potential solutions for these easier problems—for which specialization plays a vital role—and attempt to extrapolate the solutions to the point that they can be generalized. This cross-fertilization of specialization for articulating challenges to identify common problems has led to significant scientific breakthroughs. Take the example of Alan Turing and his work in computer science. By working within and across mathematics and computing, Turing formulated the concept of algorithms and is today seen as the father of artificial intelligence. Dr Hilbert himself is now recognized as one of the most influential mathematicians of the twentieth century.

If we now move away from problems within a field and to today's grand challenges formulated within the SDGs, we can see that the solutions to grand challenges require sustaining changes not just in the behaviors of individuals and businesses, but also in social interactions and systems that govern society. Only the combination of those will allow us to enact potential solutions. The wide scope of such challenges thus involves a huge array of actors with pluralistic viewpoints and interests.

Indeed, the nature of grand challenges and the pathways to solve them are comprised of multiple wicked problems—problems which traditional processes cannot resolve as they have multiple causes which are difficult to describe. What is more, the right answer only becomes obvious once the right answer emerges (Camillus, 2008). Poverty is a quintessential example of a wicked problem—how do we alleviate poverty? Why does poverty in the United States, India, Germany, China, Fiji, and Pakistan look different? Why do different countries have different methods of poverty alleviation? Why do some measures work in one country or for one group of people while they have no or even the opposite effect in others?

In 1973, Professors Horst Rittel and Melvin Webber from the University of California Berkeley, introduced the concept of wicked problems. They identified 10 characteristics of a wicked problem:

i. "*There is no definitive formulation of a wicked problem*" (Rittel & Webber, 1973, p. 161). In most instances, developing the solution for a problem first requires understanding the problem, which then elicits an iterative process of identifying potential solutions based on the available information. In the case of a wicked problem, understanding the problem is a function of the potential solutions. In short, defining a wicked problem requires an exhaustive conceptualization of all potential solutions to the currently undefined problem. This may seem paradoxical, but the wicked problem demands developing understanding of potential solutions and the problem in parallel to avoid implementing solutions that exacerbate rather than solve the problem. Thus, how the wicked problem is understood presents significant challenges for implementing a solution.

While this is challenging to implement, it is a crucial step in solving wicked problems as once a problem is defined, it sets the course and direction for its solution. Take poverty as an example. Much of the development community is faced with questions surrounding the interlinkages between poverty and crime. Specifically, does poverty cause crime or does crime cause poverty? (e.g. Anser et al., 2020). If we take the position that crime causes poverty, then 'reduce crime' becomes a pointed solution. This in turn however alienates consideration and thus any potential solutions that perceive poverty as the cause of crime. Moreover, if we then point to poor policing practices as a contributing factor for the lack of crime rate reduction, then 'enhancing policing' becomes another potential solution. If we then take it one step further and identify a lack of funding as a barrier to enhancing police work then 'fund policing' becomes an additional pointed solution. This can continue on and on until the initial problem of alleviating poverty becomes obfuscated by an overemphasis on crime reduction or police funding. Thus, the root of poverty, in any given area, cannot be understood without understanding the context—poverty alleviation in one area does not per se translate to alleviating poverty in another context. Moreover, the process of excluding potential problems early on in the process does not only make it harder to solve wicked problems but it potentially leads to an increae in the problem that one aims to solve.

ii. "*Wicked problems have no stopping rule*" (Rittel & Webber, 1973, p. 162). In contrast to tame problems, that is, problems for which we have set procedures that can be translated to different contexts, wicked problems have no endogenous end point. As mentioned above, since wicked problems demand developing an understanding of the problem and solutions in parallel, those who seek to solve society's wicked problems stop due to end points exogenous to the problem in question, such as externally imposed financial or time constraints. Let us take the construction of a bridge as an example of a tame problem. By no means an easy feat, the process of constructing a bridge follows set procedures provided through industrial and structural engineering. The underlying approach to the construction of a bridge in India is the same as construction of a bridge in Germany. Similarly, the stopping rule is clear. The bridge is complete when safety measures and structural integrity is achieved. Conversely, efforts to alleviate poverty do not have a clear and specific end point. "Zero poverty" is hardly an actionable stopping point, not least given the relative and evolving nature of poverty.

iii. "*Solutions to wicked problems are not true-false, but good-or-bad*" (Rittel & Webber, 1973, p. 162). The complexity and context specificity of a wicked problem means that there are no true or false solutions. In contrast to the tame problem, there are no set procedures against which solutions can be deemed true, false, or correct. Rather, when assessing solutions to wicked problems, terms like good, bad, satisficing, good enough, better, or worse are used. The comparative nature of these terms for assessment is because of the subjectivity with which equally 'qualified' parties might judge a given solution. For example, the set of procedures for constructing a bridge means that proposals for bridge construction can be deemed correct. When assessing solutions for the reduction of poverty, then choosing to focus on crime reduction cannot be deemed true, false, or correct, but rather better, worse, or good, depending on the person or persons doing the assessment. In fact, this subjectivity and plurality of opinions contributes to the elusiveness of many solutions.

iv. "*There is no immediate and no ultimate test of a solution to a wicked problem*" (Rittel & Webber, 1973, p. 163). The subjective, complex, and context-specific nature of wicked problems means that it is extremely difficult to establish a test for a solution or attempted solution. Similar to the above point, the lack of set procedures means that there is no set approach for testing a solution's success (or lack thereof). A set of procedures may be developed by the parties attempting to address the problem (such as documents outlining desired outcomes or deliverables) but the validity of these procedures is a function of the parties developing the procedures rather than the nature of the problem itself. For example, a charity, NGO, or social enterprise wins a grant to implement a project with the aim of alleviating poverty. The project aims do so by providing entrepreneurial skill building to a rural village or marginalized demographic and has 'increased local enterprise creation' as one of its deliverables. As a precondition for the grant, let's say the funding body wants to see 'a 10% reduction of unemployment'. In the first instance, there is no way to be certain that increased local enterprise creation will lead to a 10% reduction of unemployment. When implementing solutions for wicked problems, there are successive waves of implications that are not temporally bound, meaning that the outcomes or deliverables set forth by the parties involved may not align with the reality of the impact of the solutions. Enterprises could be created and then fail, the effects of entrepreneurial skill building could emerge from a successive generation rather than the individuals who participated in skill building workshops (parents could teach their children or vice versa and then they eventually create an enterprise), those who engaged in the skill building could move away, or new entrepreneurs could become victims of crimes of jealousy. In short, (attempted) solutions to wicked problems may have outcomes which cannot be foreseen and thus cannot be tested until they have played out. As time goes on, solutions can have negative consequences which depart drastically from the intended consequences when the (attempted) solution was first implemented.

v. "*Every solution to a wicked problem is a 'one-shot operation'; because there is no opportunity to learn by trial-and-error, every attempt counts significantly*" (Rittel & Webber, 1973, p. 163). When trying to address wicked problems, the lack of immediate tests and set procedures means that the implications of (attempted) solutions are unknown. Due to the interlinkages that constitute the wicked problem, each attempted solution has reverberative effects that impact the interconnections of the problem itself. For instance, a poverty alleviation project cannot be implemented, analyzed, undone, and tried again differently. The implementation of a solution and the subsequent outcomes alters the context within which the next iteration of a solution is enacted. Thus, every attempted solution needs to be carefully considered and counts significantly because the parameters of a problem are impacted by its s (attempted) solutions.

vi. "*Wicked problems do not have an enumerable (or an exhaustively describable) set of potential solutions, nor is there a well-described set of permissible operations that may be incorporated into the plan*" (Rittel & Webber, 1973, p. 164). The tame problem (e.g. bridge construction) has an exhaustive set of permissible operations. For example, bridges can be built in multiple ways so long as they adhere to the mathematical and physical principles which maintain its structural integrity and allows it to carry the necessary weight. As such, it is finitely bounded by the laws of physics. This is not so for the wicked problem. Due to its subjectivity and context specificity, the wicked problem is bounded only by the imagination of the parties searching for a solution. Following the preceding prepositions, the lack of set procedures is equally true for the procedures for determining the extent to which an exhaustive number of solutions have been considered. Just because no solution has been found doesn't mean there is no solution. Similarly, it is entirely possible that solutions are ambivalent—they are both good and bad simultaneously. Even if solutions emerge, more successful options might be feasible. Furthermore, following point i), poorly understood problems lead to poor determinability of solutions and the permissible operations that we may incorporate. For wicked problems, the rules of the game are a social construction rather than a phenomenal reality of the problem. That is, any potential solution could become a legitimate possibility. For example, in responding to the problem of poverty, if we identify corruption as a significant cause of poverty, how should we go about reducing corruption? Should we put all those found to be corrupt in prison? Should we redefine corruption so there is less corruption, by definition, though it remains the same in effect? Do we seek to strengthen the role of governance institutions, which is an increasingly adopted strategy (e.g. Andersen, 2009)? As we reduce corruption, do we keep some corruption? Research suggests that there is an optimal level of corruption for maximizing growth (Dzhumashev, 2014). Thus, effective solutions require a balance of normativity (what we should do) and positivity (what can be done), which ultimately involves judgement calls from those parties enacting the solutions.

vii. "*Every wicked problem is essentially unique*" (Rittel & Webber, 1973, p. 164). The nature of wicked problems means that there are always specific elements that distinguish them from one another and makes general solutions unattainable. While wicked problems might seem similar, it's not possible to determine whether a successful solution in one context can be implemented in another context with the same success. When implementing approaches to poverty alleviation, they might not work across contexts due to differences in culture or religion. For instance, if we seek to address poverty through a loan-based system in the United States (e.g., microcredits), the same approach might not be implementable in some countries due to Islamic Banking principles.

viii. "*Every wicked problem can be considered to be a symptom of another problem*" (Rittel & Webber, 1973, p. 165). In the case of the wicked problem, we cannot easily identify causality. In fact, a common trap of the wicked problem is misidentification of causality and correlation. If we think back to the interlinkages between crime and poverty, the direction of causality is unclear. Does crime cause poverty or does poverty cause crime? There is certainly a correlation. That is, they move in coordination with one another. Where we see high poverty, we can expect to see high crime. Without clear causality, the wicked problem is intertwined with another problem and the wicked problem in question may be understood as a symptom of a problem in itself.

ix. "*The existence of a discrepancy representing a wicked problem can be explained in numerous ways. The choice of explanation determines the nature of the problem's resolution*" (Rittel & Webber, 1973, p. 166). Poverty can be explained by greed, by corruption, poor economic policies, poor judicial policies, labor force shortages, poor education, and so on. As laid out in point i, each explanation sets the course and direction for potential solutions. How can we determine which one is 'correct' (point iii)? In searching for a solution, we build our understanding of an effective outcome by hypothesizing the role of interconnected variables and how these variables can be manipulated to achieve a desired state. Thus if we assume crime explains poverty, the police force would receive funding to enhance policing. Through this enhanced policing, there is a reduction in low-level crime, we may see an increase in Gross Domestic Product (GDP), but a stagnation in the Gini coefficient (the statistical dispersion of wealth inequality). Has poverty been alleviated through enhanced funding for the police? In this case, the answer is it depends on what is measured. One assessment could be the alleviation of poverty has been successful from a macro perspective (i.e. a higher national GDP). Thus, if the assessor of the solutions chooses to explain the outcome as a success at the macro level, then the solution to the problem becomes a macro level question.

x. "*The planner has no right to be wrong*" (Rittel & Webber, 1973, p. 166). As set out in the preceding 9 points, the multiplicity of directions for a potential solution to the wicked problem means that the parties developing solutions aim only to improve some aspect of the social world. That is, in seeking solutions, we are not per se looking for the definitive causes of a wicked problem. Providing solutions to poverty, for example, does not mean identifying an exhaustive list of the causes of poverty. It would certainly help to have an exhaustive list, but searching for solutions is not to searching for a theory of everything.

In sum, the aim and solutions for wicked problems are defined by the plurality of the social contexts within which they emerge. Plurality regarding their definition, their solutions, and their appraisal. Wicked problems and grand challenges are similar in their pluralism but differ in their scale and scope. As the world becomes more intertwined, tackling the wicked problems of our time is paramount for surmounting the grand challenges of our time.

1.2 Context of Our Data

Tackling grand challenges require global collaborative effort whilst keeping local context in mind. Doing so requires identifying the complex underpinnings of cultural and social issues, testing context specific solutions, and extrapolating it globally. For the purpose of this book, we aim to untangle these and put forward pathways by building on social entrepreneurship. Social entrepreneurship is a practice-led phenomenon that operates at the micro, meso, and macro levels of society. It is therefore uniquely positioned, as a tool, to address wicked problems and grand challenges. However, like all tools, achieving socially desirable outcomes from social entrepreneurship is contingent on the context within which it is employed. In particular, which problems social entrepreneurs aim to solve and the strategies adopted within their environment. To this end, a nuanced perspective can help demarcate the role of social entrepreneurship in addressing grand challenges through a discussion of the various implications of social entrepreneurship.

To generate insights into the role of social entrepreneurship within grand challenges and the SDGs, we combine well-known examples of social entrepreneurs who have created social change, with our own empirical data of social entrepreneurs collected during the COVID-19 pandemic. In doing so, we present the role of social entrepreneurs as both initiators of and responders to disruption. Our data was collected in the Netherlands and the United Kingdom; two countries consistently ranked highly in entrepreneurial culture (Acs et al., 2017, 2020; Bosma et al., 2021). Our 17 participants were interviewed at various points in the COVID-19 pandemic, 9 of which kept diaries throughout the pandemic and were interviewed again after 10 months of diary writing.

1.3 How This Book is Organized

This book is organized into six chapters that build up our conceptualization of social entrepreneurship within the context of grand challenges and the SDGs step-by-step. Our conceptual work is supported and illustrated through our case studies and publicly available examples.

Chapter 2 serves to introduce the reader to the literature on social entrepreneurship. We highlight the extant knowledge regarding how social entrepreneurship can tackle grand challenges and deal with crises. We carve out the gaps in the current literature; particularly, we point to the need for understanding the role of space, institutions, systems and the imaginary to fully capture the role of social entrepreneur(ship) to effectively address the challenges of our times. Borrowing from the institutional analysis literature (e.g. Bouilloud et al., 2020; Castoriadis, 1992, 1997) we incorporate the social imaginary to provide a 'beyond functionalist' view of institutions (Castoriadis, 1997). The social imaginary refers to the ability of people to represent beyond what can be seen, and this makes up a fundamental process with which people make sense of their environment. The social imaginary allows us to engage more deeply with the capacity of social entrepreneur(ship) to influence symbolic inertia for change.

Chapter 3 provides readers with an in-depth understanding of the emergence and behavior of systems to better conceptualize the complexities of society. In so doing, we lay the foundation of the book by illustrating how complex societal problems might emerge and promulgate. While we recognize the importance of action and agency from the micro-level (i.e. social entrepreneurs), we implement Luhmann's systems theory (Luhmann, 1982) as a theoretical lens through which to examine modern society, and lay the groundwork for understanding the complexities which give rise to grand challenges and restructure the impetus for positive societal change. Based on Luhmann's work, we highlight the varying methods of communication that can be implemented to understand and address disruptions at multiple societal layers, such as those caused by the COVID 19 pandemic. To best introduce this process, we induce the ordonomic framework (Pies et al., 2009) to illustrate the interdependencies between institutions and actors as a mechanism through which individual actors communicate with the social systems of society. Ordonomics engages Luhmann's theory of social system and identifies three levels of interaction within a social system (Pies et al., 2009). The first level, the basic game, is where interactions that form society are conducted. The second level, the meta game, is where institutions are created to promote collaborative social structures. The third level, the meta meta game, is where ideas surrounding shared perception and experiences are promulgated in pursuit of joint movement toward institutional change (Pies et al., 2010). The multilayered framework of ordonomics advocates the importance of the relationship between institutions and perceptions, and is thus uniquely qualified to build from the symbolic and functional institutional analysis induced in Chap. 2. This in turn serves us to discuss why rules are needed, how they emerge, and how they link to the wider structures of society.

Chapter 4 induces the COVID-19 lockdowns as a case analysis for demonstrating the ways in which space shapes and is shaped by the imagination. We conjecture that disruption to space has significant implications on the behavior, both symbolic and physical, of individual actors (i.e. social entrepreneurs). Through this illustrative case, we demonstrate how spatial configuration can be an additional tool for communicating change and addressing grand challenges beyond the physical space by influencing the patterns of communication. As such, Chap. 4 analyses the impact of spatial disruption as one of the many forms of disruption facing society, which social entrepreneur(ship) navigates through innovative methods of articulation. Building upon the previous two chapters, we argue that the attribution of meaning and symbolic communication is central to the processes by which space subsumes different roles and acts as an additional method of communicating value to affect systems change. To do so, we discuss the materiality of space as a fundamental component for mediating the social interactions that may emerge in a space. Additionally, this chapter presents an overview of netnographic (Kozinets, 2002) and practice tracing (Pouliot, 2015) methodologies as vital epistemological tools for future researchers interested in critically analyzing the dynamic relationships between social and material elements of space, subsequent spatial configurations, meaning associated with new configurations, and behavioral changes that arise within space.

Chapter 5 deconstructs the social entrepreneurial process as a multilevel process of disruption. Building on the foundations set forth in Chaps. 1,2,3, and 4, Chapter 5 utilizes the lens of social entrepreneurship, particularly the social innovation model of social entrepreneurship to demonstrate the multiple layers of society at which social entrepreneurship, and by extension, individual actors disrupt societal patterns of communication. In particular, this chapter aims to analyze how individual agents have the capacity to incorporate varying methods of communication (such as space or the imagination) to initiate change and tackle wicked problems. Further, we induce the concept of ambivalence (Zeyen & Beckmann, 2018) as an additional lens for conceptualizing social entrepreneurship, not as a panacea for societal problems, but as a tool for addressing wicked problems whose efficacy is a function of the problem it is used to address.

Chapter 6 induces the concept of the type III error (Kimball, 1957) as a phenomenological outcome of communication patterns which obfuscate the path towards grand challenges and exacerbate wicked problems rather than solve them. We then present in-depth thought experiments through which readers may implement the theoretical constructs built through the preceding chapters. In doing so, Chap. 6 comments on practical examples of social entrepreneurs who have begun addressing grand challenges by reorienting the patterns of communication within society to learn from errors of the third kind to enable systems to change themselves. These examples showcase how wicked problems and grand challenges (including the COVID-19 pandemic, climate crises, and inequalities) can be addressed at each of society's strata while incorporating symbolic and less tangible methods of communication. Additionally, examining such cases from an external and de novo perspective (e.g. Luhmann's systems theory) allows us to clearly view inflection points where errors of the third kind could be avoided. Our journey ends with empirical examples which can be linked to daily life, in respect to how grand challenges and wicked problems are addressed through innovative methods of communication, which extend beyond the physical, and engage with the imaginary to address the fundamental root of complex problems. This enables readers to re-examine their understandings of the Sustainable Development Goals to better identify and ameliorate communicative roadblocks which ultimately obfuscate problem identification and promulgate grand challenges.

References

Acs, Z., Szerb, L., & Autio, E. (2017). The global entrepreneurship index. In *Global entrepreneurship and development index 2016* (pp. 19–38). Springer.

Acs, Z., Szerb, L., Lafuente, E., & Márkus, G. (2020). The global entrepreneurship index. In *Global entrepreneurship and development index 2019*. The Global Entrepreneurship and Development Institute.

Andersen, T. B. (2009). E-Government as an anti-corruption strategy. *Information Economics and policy, 21*(3), 201–210.

Anser, M. K., Yousaf, Z., Nassani, A. A., Alotaibi, S. M., Kabbani, A., & Zaman, K. (2020). Dynamic linkages between poverty, inequality, crime, and social expenditures in a panel of 16 countries: two-step GMM estimates. *Journal of Economic Structures, 9*(1), 1–25.

Bacq, S., Geoghegan, W., Josefy, M., Stevenson, R., & Williams, T. A. (2020). The COVID-19 Virtual Idea Blitz: Marshaling social entrepreneurship to rapidly respond to urgent grand challenges. *Business Horizons, 63*(6), 705–723.

Bosma, N., Hill, S., Ionescu-Somers, A., Kelley, D., Guerrero, M., & Schott, T. (2021). *Global entrepreneurship monitor 2020/2021 global report*. Global Entrepreneurship Research Association.

Bouilloud, J. P., Perezts, M., Viale, T., & Schaepelynck, V. (2020). Beyond the stable image of institutions: Using institutional analysis to tackle classic questions in institutional theory. *Organization Studies, 41*(2), 153–174.

Camillus, J. C. (2008). "Strategy as a wicked problem". *Harvard business review, 86*(5), 98–101.

Castoriadis, C. (1992). Logic, imagination, reflection. *American Imago, 49*(1), 3–33.

Castoriadis, C. (1997). *The imaginary institution of society.* Mit Press.

Dzhumashev, R. (2014). Corruption and growth: The role of governance, public spending, and economic development. *Economic Modelling, 37*, 202–215.

Ferraro, F., Etzion, D., & Gehman, J. (2015). "Tackling grand challenges pragmatically: Robust action revisited". *Organization Studies, 36*(3): 363–390.

George, G., Howard-Grenville, J., Joshi, A., & Tihanyi, L. (2016). Understanding and tackling societal grand challenges through management research. *Academy of Management Journal, 59*(6), 1880–1895.

Hilbert, D. (1902). Mathematical problems. *Bulletin of the American Mathematical Society, 8*(10), 437–479.

Kimball, A. W. (1957). Errors of the third kind in statistical consulting. *Journal of the American Statistical Association, 52*(278), 133–142.

Kozinets, R. V. (2002). "The field behind the screen: Using netnography for marketing research in online communities". *Journal of marketing research, 39*(1), 61–72.

Kraus, S., Clauss, T., Breier, M., Gast, J., Zardini, A., & Tiberius, V. (2020). "The economics of COVID-19: initial empirical evidence on how family firms in five European countries cope with the corona crisis". *International Journal of Entrepreneurial Behavior & Research.*

Luhmann, N. (1982). The world society as a social system, Int. J. General Systems *8*, 131–138.

Pies, I., Hielscher, S., & Beckmann, M. (2009). Moral commitments and the societal role of business: An ordonomic approach to corporate citizenship. *Business Ethics Quarterly, 19*(3), 375–401.

Pies, I., Beckmann, M., & Hielscher, S. (2010). Value creation, management competencies, and global corporate citizenship: An ordonomic approach to business ethics in the age of globalization. *Journal of Business Ethics, 94*(2), 265–278.

Pouliot, V. (2015). "Practice tracing". Process tracing: From metaphor to analytic tool, 237–259.

Rittel, H. W., & Webber, M. M. (1973). Dilemmas in a general theory of planning. *Policy Sciences, 4*(2), 155–169.

United Nations General Assembly (UNGA). (2015). Transforming our world: the 2030 Agenda for Sustainable Development, Resolution adopted by the General Assembly on 25 September 2015. A/RES/70/1 21 October 2015. New York: United Nations.

United Nations General Assembly (UNGA). (2021). The Sustainable Development Goals Report 2021. https://unstats.un.org/sdgs/report/2021/

Van Wijk, J., Zietsma, C., Dorado, S., De Bakker, F. G., & Marti, I. (2019). Social innovation: Integrating micro, meso, and macro level insights from institutional theory. *Business & Society, 58*(5), 887–918.

World Health Organization (WHO). (2020). Who, coronvirus disease (COVID-19) outbreak, available at: https://www.who.int/emergencies/diseases/novel-oronavirus-2019

Zeyen, A., & Beckmann, M. (2018). *Social entrepreneurship and business ethics: Understanding the contribution and normative ambivalence of purpose-driven venturing*. Routledge.

CHAPTER 2

Social Entrepreneurship, Grand Challenges and Crisis: What We Know So Far

Abstract Social entrepreneurship is a form of entrepreneurship that utilizes entrepreneurial process to create long-lasting societal change. In this chapter, we briefly outline the status quo of the social entrepreneurship literature while specifically focusing on our current understanding of social entrepreneurship in the context of crises and grand challenges. We then look at the extant literature examining the role of social entrepreneurship in crises and how this enhances our insight into the role of social entrepreneurship for addressing societal grand challenges.

Keywords Crisis • Social entrepreneurship • Grand challenges • Social imaginary • innovation

Give a man a fish and you feed him for a day. Teach him how to fish and you feed him for a lifetime
—Proverb

2.1 A Brief Journey Through the History of Entrepreneurship

As many scholars delineate it from commercial entrepreneurship to carve out its uniqueness (Dees, 1998; Dees & Anderson, 2006; Nicholls, 2009; Stephan et al., 2015), we will briefly outline some of the key stages within

E. Costales, A. Zeyen, *Social Entrepreneurship and Grand Challenges*, https://doi.org/10.1007/978-3-031-07450-9_2

the development of the concept of entrepreneurship. Moreover, in order to fully understand social entrepreneurship, it is important to understand its umbrella term.

The concept of entrepreneurship dates back over 250 years. In his 1776 work *An Inquiry Into the Nature and Causes of the Wealth of Nations*, Adam Smith referred to the entrepreneur as one who changes demand into supply. The Wealth of Nations analyzes the operations of an economy which at the time was heavily agrarian and manufactural. Smith identified three factors necessary to produce commodities: land, labor, and capital. In Smith's conceptualization, such combinations are a strategic endeavor which serve various economic functions in society. While he does not use the term entrepreneurship, we can interpret these strategic endeavors as entrepreneurship.

Jean-Baptiste Say, the nineteenth century French economist credited with defining the term entrepreneurship, described the entrepreneur as one who moves economic resources from areas of low yield to ones of greater yield (Say, 1846).[1] In his 1848 work *Principles of Political Economy with some of their Applications to Social Philosophy*, John Stuart Mill posited that entrepreneurs constitute a fourth factor of production, in addition to labor, land, and capital. Entrepreneurs reorient divisions of labor, promote specialization, and enhance efficiency. In his view, entrepreneurs are those individuals who assume the risks and management of enterprise creation. Thus, for Mill, fundamental to the entrepreneur is their risk-taking ability and capacity for organizing.

Nearly a century later, the economist most closely associated with modern entrepreneurship, Joseph Schumpeter, introduced an innovation theory of entrepreneurship, whereby innovation forms the central tenet of entrepreneurship (Schumpeter, 1939). For Schumpeter, an entrepreneur's organizational capacity and risk-acceptance is of significantly less importance than their innovative capacity. Schumpeter introduced the process of *Creative Destruction* as "...[an] essential aspect of capitalism" (p. 83). This process involves mechanisms of innovation in production or service delivery which consistently leads to the replacement of the old. This "perennial gale" of creative destruction brings with it a new type of competition: "...competition from the new commodity, the new technology, the new source of supply, *the new type of organization*..." (p. 84, *our*

[1] This was built on Richard Cantillon's definition from his 1732 book *Essay on the Nature of Commerce in General*

emphasis). From this perspective, innovation is primarily a disruptive activity whereby less efficient patterns of production are supplanted by more efficient combinations of the factors of production.

In Schumpeter's view, invention does not per se lead to innovation, and innovation does not require invention. As Schumpeter puts it "the entrepreneur and his function are not difficult to conceptualize: the defining characteristic is simply the doing of things that are already being done in a new way (innovation). It is but natural, and in fact it is an advantage, that such a definition does not draw any sharp line between what is and what is not 'enterprise'" (Schumpeter, 1947, p. 151).

Along this Schumpeterian perspective, entrepreneurs are not required to cause change, rather they exploit the opportunities that change creates (Drucker, 1985, 2012). The dynamic social context within which entrepreneurs operate (which is further dissected in Chap. 3) results in a high velocity of change where values shift at the micro, meso, and macro levels. The emergence of multiple branches of entrepreneurship is a manifestation of such multi-level changes. As we continue through this book, we maintain the Schumpeterian view of entrepreneurship.

2.2 The Emergence of Social Entrepreneurship: Business Beyond the Profit Motive

Over the last 25 years, social entrepreneurship has emerged as a concept in academia and practice. To be clear, this does not mean that social entrepreneurship did not previously exist, but rather that it was not coined thus. In fact, some of the most widely referenced examples of early social entrepreneurial activity are the works of Maria Montessori in early childcare and Florence Nightingale for reforming nursing (Zeyen & Beckmann, 2018).

However, the shift to defining and attempting to formalize social entrepreneurship as a concept supported its legitimation as a distinct type of entrepreneuring. Specifically, it is a method of solving social problems that is more than a form of charity (Soros, 2000) but rather employs (social) innovation to tackle often complex societal problems (Dacin et al., 2011). Historically, solving social problems came in the form of charity through religious institutions (Rushton, 2001), community structures (Branzei et al., 2018), or charitable organizations (Dees, 2012).

At its core, social entrepreneurship aims to solve or alleviate societal problems. Figure 2.1 shows a simplified depiction of where social entrepreneurship fits within a society's mechanisms of social innovation. The checkered arrows denote the multi-directionality of the interactions between the market, state, and social entrepreneurship as they observe and learn from one another. While the market and state alone, or in combination, can be very potent tools to solve societal problems, there are nonetheless societal issues that are either addressed inefficiently or not at all by the market and state (e.g., Zeyen et al., 2013). Here, social entrepreneurship can operate as a tool to provide problem solutions to those market or state inefficiencies or gaps. They do so through the use of (social) innovation. This is why Felix Oldenburg coined the notion that social entrepreneurs operate as a society's research and development department (Oldenburg, 2011).

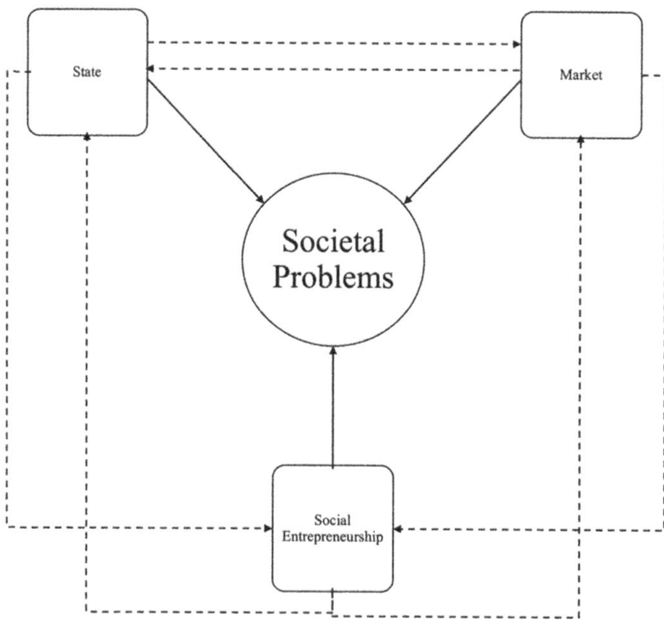

Fig. 2.1 Social Entrepreneurship's position within society's mechanisms of social innovation

To illustrate, we draw on the example of Beth, a social entrepreneur operating in Amsterdam who runs a social venture pushing for greater accessibility around the city, as she talks about the inception of her venture:

> As a disabled person, and losing my mobility, I kind of realized that even though there were some places I could find that were step free or accessible in other ways, I didn't really know where I could go, not just in Amsterdam, but it really—I know the feeling of disappointment and helplessness when you get somewhere and you can't get in and it ruins your day. And then I kind of realized that I couldn't be the only one with this problem. So I started making a list on my phone of places I knew to be accessible... [the issue] is definitely the fact that the Netherlands doesn't have the right regulations to ensure that there's like a minimum standard for accessibility, but on the other hand, I definitely think its also in some cases people not following the rules

The shortcomings of the market and state that Beth describes reflects how she, as a social entrepreneur, was spurred to action by observing the inefficiencies of the market (business owners not fully incentivized to adhere to rules of accessibility) and state (inefficient regulations to ensure standard of accessibility), through her own lived experiences. To address these dual inefficiencies, Beth began with a social media campaign to promote businesses that are inclusively accessible and nudge clientele (disabled and otherwise) towards these businesses. She coupled this campaign with in-person consulting to educate business owners on what it means to be accessible. In this way, Beth leveraged the market mechanism to incentivize business owners to adhere to the (informal) rules of accessibility. In parallel, Beth has begun engaging with local policymakers to highlight the inefficiencies of the current regulations and leverage the state mechanism to formalize additional rules of accessibility.

The social entrepreneurship literature is full of accounts of how social entrepreneurs have created large scale system change through providing a new template for tackling certain societal issues or by providing policy changes or enabling public discussions of previously overlooked or understated problems (Datta & Gailey, 2012; Thompson & Doherty, 2006; Zeyen et al., 2014). The literature further highlights the embedded nature of social entrepreneurs (Seelos et al., 2011). As our example above shows, social entrepreneurs build their ventures on personal, professional, or vicarious experience (Corner & Ho, 2010; Hockerts, 2017; Shaw &

Carter, 2007). This deeply embedded nature of their problem-solving approach allows them to (i) better understand the problem and its causes and (ii) develop solutions that have the user or beneficiary in mind. The latter is often only feasible because they are a member of the community they aim to serve or have worked within that community previously. While our examples showcase social issues, social entrepreneurship is not limited to social issues, as it also includes environmental issues. Here, again social entrepreneurs (such as the documentarians of the ALBATROS documentary or Al Harris, founder of Blue Ventures), build on their lived experience and professional expertise of environmental challenges to provide solutions.

We would like to highlight that society-level change—often referred to as social change (Hietschold et al., 2019)—can only be achieved by linking the individual (micro), organizational (meso) and system (macro) levels of society. However, if we stay with the assumption that personal embeddedness is a key feature and factor in identifying solutions with social change potential, then the question of what happens if the "known" gets disrupted arises. The COVID-19 pandemic created a circumstance that was unprecedented and therefore no social entrepreneur could build on their personal or professional experience and expertise in order to address it. Yet, we have seen many social entrepreneurs "step up" and provide vital resources for the community. For instance, Sally, a social entrepreneur operating in London who runs a social venture advocating the employability of persons with disabilities, provided vital resources for her community during the COVID-19 pandemic:

> For [venture] I was working with a care organization to get the volunteers trialing everything with learning disabled adults, but due to the lockdowns they weren't working face-to-face, everything was remote. So there were no more volunteers for [venture]...through [venture] contacts, I've still been doing social entrepreneurial stuff with [a community interest company]. Instead of making meals with [venture] I do outreach stuff like feeding—making meals for the community out of a church that are then delivered to locals

While the COVID-19 lockdowns had significant negative impacts on Sally's ability to continue running her own venture, she shifted her attention to community needs that were inefficiently addressed by the market and the state, as she describes:

> what seems to be the case is that quite a lot of organizations, and certainly because of COVID and the lockdowns, have started doing is, you know, projects helping those vulnerable people, but actually we could do a lot more if people were trying to work together rather than everybody just working in their own little silos. So that's where I can make more of an impact with [community interest company] and not just being another one of these organizations doing just a little bit. If we can coordinate everybody, then actually we'll have a better impact than what's currently going on.

The inefficiencies of the market and state, against the backdrop of the COVID-19 lockdowns, which Sally describes incentivized her to provide additional resources that vulnerable persons were simply not able to receive through the market and state mechanisms. Indeed, from the market, organizations were incentivized to continue operating in siloed mentalities which did not fully capture the impact necessary to make enough of a difference. From the state perspective, while the lockdowns were enacted from the perspective of public health, they were not coupled with provisions for ensuring that the people most impacted would have access to vital things, such as food. Based on these observations, Sally, as a social entrepreneur, was spurred to fill in these gaps in a similar way to the work she was doing with her venture prior to the COVID-19 pandemic.

In a similar vein, Winona, a social entrepreneur running a social venture in Amsterdam which transforms people's work environments to allow them to perform their jobs in the most sustainable and fulfilling way, opted to provide free consultation for a social enterprise, SAW (pseudonym) focusing on labor market discrimination:

> The last few months have been quite tumultuous. Since corona started in the Netherlands we had a lockdown in March…With the lockdown I couldn't see any client face-to-face anymore. Frankly, that was a big blow… One good thing is that I've been doing some work with [SAW] and I've connected with people I might not have ever met. [SAW] has applied for the government aid, and I have too, but it has still not resulted in anything, so if I can help them while I figure out how to move forward then they can keep supporting the people they want to support. It doesn't cover any costs, but the work that I've done the last few weeks is helping the cohort with how to prepare, pitch to the job market, and I see them doing the work. I've also been helping some students who are in their first year of university. They need to do a project for a company and probably because of corona

> they have not been able to connect with anyone. So I thought they can have a look at my enterprise and make some recommendations

Winona has opted to fill the gap left by the market and the state through supporting an existing social enterprise. She addresses the inefficiencies of the state felt by both her and SAW (not receiving government aid) by shifting her focus to offering in-kind aid to support SAW's social mission. SAW's emphasis on labor market discrimination aimed to address the inefficiencies of the market under normal circumstances. The economic impacts of COVID (such as furlough, layoffs, and supply chain troubles) enhanced this market inefficiency and Winona's observation of this deficiency spurred her to act in the best way she knew how. At the same time, she sought to maintain a semblance of normalcy by supporting university students whose educational journeys were impacted by the COVID-19 lockdowns.

In order to better understand the role of social entrepreneurs and their ventures in crisis, we will briefly review the extant research and highlight current gaps. We incorporate the concept of the social imaginary as a means of further illustrating the impact of social entrepreneurially involvement for navigating disruptions caused by crises.

2.3 Social Entrepreneurship and Crisis

Borrowing from institutional analysis (Castoriadis, 1977) we induce the social imaginary (see Castoriadis, 1987) as a lens for illustrating the impact of social entrepreneurship during crisis. The social imaginary is premised on the notion of the 'radical imaginary' (Castoriadis, 1987) which accounts for individual autonomy; capacity for rationally pursuing one's goals; and the interrelation between individual behavior, social context, individual needs, and societal needs, beyond traditional economic functions. It is the radical imaginary which enables people to impart meaning onto something which may deviate from its traditional use. The social imaginary involves the socialized capacity of the radical imaginary and human beings to represent beyond empirical fact, and constitutes a fundamental link between individuals and their environments (see Patalano, 2007). The relative detachment from empirical validation and ability to create meaning beyond what has already been created, promoted by the concept of the social imaginary (Patalano, 2007), contributes to an understanding of how social entrepreneurs contribute to navigating crisis.

What do we understand by a crisis? Crisis refers to a disruptive situation which requires urgent decision making, system reconfiguration, involves extreme uncertainty, and lays bare existing power asymmetries (Shrivastava, 1993; Moerschell & Novak, 2020). Here, extant literature examining social entrepreneurship in the context of natural disasters (e.g. Dutta, 2017; Chamlee-Wright & Storr, 2010; Yu, 2016; Ibrahim & El Ebrashi, 2017) paints an optimistic picture of how the constitutive behavior of social entrepreneurs helps navigate crisis. For example, social entrepreneurs have a unique understanding of the local markets and social structures, which enable them to accurately assess the specific needs of the impacted community, and develop social services to meet these needs (Ibrahim & El Ebrashi, 2017). Similarly, Dutta (2017) points out that social entrepreneurship organizes collective goods and reorients the purpose of spaces through the founding of "homeless shelters, soup kitchens, voluntary fire departments, local youth groups, and other such locally organized nonprofit human services organizations" (p.3). Further, Barbera-Tomas and colleagues (2019) show that social entrepreneurs engage in symbolic work to purposely invoke shock to inspire people to work towards a desired goal. To illicit changes in behavior to avoid single use plastic, social entrepreneurs used a picture of a dead Albatross chick with plastic in its stomach as a means of framing the damaging effects of single use plastic in a way that resonates with people's daily lives, despite not living near an ocean (see Barberá-Tomás et al., 2019, p. 1794).

A fundamental challenge posed by crisis is one of collective action (Chamlee-Wright & Storr, 2009; Dutta, 2017). Returning to the foundations of wicked problems from Chap. 1, crises present a complex array of disruptions to the status quo which introduce multiple wicked problem such as poverty, crime, or poor water quality. In many instances of crisis, humanitarian efforts are comprised of voluntary and philanthropic initiatives (e.g. Yu, 2016; Chamlee-Wright & Storr, 2014), which may exacerbate challenges to organization by relying on external actors and inviting confusing post-disaster policy (see Chamlee-Wright, 2007). The uncertainty created by crises further enhances the tension between the social imaginary (e.g. collective meanings imparted on shared realities) and the resource-constrained place (Wright et al., 2020). That is, if social spaces prior to a crisis (let's say a coffee shop or a social club) were destroyed during a hurricane or became unusable due to some other crisis, then the collective meaning of what remains is in tension with the pre-crisis symbolic status of a given place. In short, rebuilding after crisis requires insight into the local context to rebuild the physical and symbolic elements of the affected area.

Regional embeddedness of social entrepreneurs (e.g. Dahl & Sorenson, 2012) presents stable sources of support and insight in the form of local ties and fluency regarding local structural conditions pre crisis (e.g. Seelos et al., 2011). Social entrepreneurs are thus uniquely suited for addressing local challenges of organization and recovery, due to their innovative methods of engaging the social imaginary and navigating the disrupted symbols of meaning within a local context. For example, social services provided by social entrepreneurs such as homeless shelters (Dutta, 2017) or commercial spaces reorganized as social spaces (Storr et al., 2015) act as signs of investment in an affected area (Haeffele & Craig, 2020). Thus, the efforts of social entrepreneurs signal to government officials, external investors, and displaced community members that the affected community is primed for rebounding (c.f. Storr et al., 2017).

As pointed out by Dutta (2017), Social entrepreneurs have the capacity to reflect on familiar space and endow it with new meaning to reconcile the imaginary with local reality through their involvement in the provision of social services (c.f. Castoriadis, 1987, 1992). In so doing, familiar spaces deviate from the expected with unforeseeable potential. For example, Chamlee-Wright and Storr (2014) show that commercial stores in the post-Katrina hurricane context provided critical services, access to information and fostered reconnection of pre-existing social networks. In these instances, different spaces act as a catalyst of meaning: as space is co-opted by people endowing it with meaning (e.g. commercial stores acting as social spaces), the salience of these meanings become embedded within the elements of the space in question and ameliorates place-based restrictions (such as resource constraints or enhanced risks). For example, churches may become spaces of economic activity and convenience stores may become spaces of social activity.

Such behaviors further develop the social imaginary by enabling local communities to address current needs and identify underlying problems. Through the efforts of social entrepreneurs (and other prosocial actors), this identification holds the potential to impart new meanings and initiate innovative processes of resilience.

2.4 Grand Challenge or Wicked Problems: Learning from Crisis

If we now turn our attention back to grand challenges, we can see that while insightful, current understandings of the role of social entrepreneurs in crises fall short to fully explain their role during the COVID-19 pandemic and for grand challenges more generally.

George et al. (2016) point out that addressing grand challenges can be characterized as uniquely management problems because solutions involve changing societal and individual behavior. As mentioned in Chap. 1, solutions also require comprehensive identification and understanding of the problem in order to provide a solution. If we look to the Sustainable Development Goals as the most prevalent grand challenges of our time, we can reinterpret grand challenges as specific ideal end conditions obstructed by one or more wicked problem(s) that, if removed, would enable societal movement towards the ideal end condition. For example, no poverty (SDG 1), reduced inequalities (SDG 10), and peace and justice (SDG 16) are ideal end conditions which are currently obstructed by the wicked problems of poverty, inequality, and conflict and injustice, respectively. With the SDGs, society has identified ideal societal conditions, however, it is unlikely the world will meet these conditions by 2030. The question we should ask ourselves is why, despite identifying ideal conditions, have we not made the necessary strides in order to move towards these end conditions?

Social entrepreneurs aim to resolve grand challenges from the bottom up. Many examples demonstrate how such ventures are able to push the SDG agenda. For instance, Cathy, a social entrepreneur based in Rotterdam, The Netherlands, runs a social venture which seeks to ameliorate labor force discrimination. They are (self professedly) working towards SDG 4 (quality education), SDG 8 (decent work and economic growth), and SDG 10 (reduced inequalities). To do this, Cathy targets the internalized stigma of the people she works with as a means of combating the underlying problem of discrimination. This is coupled with extensive IT and interviewing skills to prepare them with confidence in demonstrating their abilities as competent workers for the twenty-first century labor market. When thinking about achieving the SDGS, Cathy emphasizes the importance of taking a bottom-up approach to make meaningful social change:

> people say to me, well, you know, 'would you like to come and do it here in my country?' And I'm like, 'no, what I would like you to do is to send

> people from your community, have them come through our program, go through the process and then we will support you in setting it up in your own community, because it should be yours'. It should be relevant to the community. It shouldn't be me as a Dutch startup saying, 'you in this country, you need to do this. And you in this country needs to do that'. Right? I don't want to be any, I don't, I don't want to use philanthropy to make my impact. I just want to do shit right from the beginning and see the impact be made that way. Right? Just do the right thing from day one and start in the communities who need it

The literature on social entrepreneurship frequently highlights the focus on impact models and aims to understand how social entrepreneurs and their ventures manage to achieve these societal shifts (e.g. Santos et al., 2015; Zeyen et al., 2014). Other studies focus on how social entrepreneurship across ventures creates systemic change (e.g. Haugh & Talwar, 2016; Nicholls, 2008; Nicholls et al., 2015).

The COVID-19 crisis highlighted significant shortcomings in society's functionalities. It called into question who has value, where value comes from, the intricacies of our economic system, the role of the public sector, the private sector, and the role of space in societal interaction. What it did not call into question is our ideal end conditions. In short, society's wicked problems are exacerbated by crises, but grand challenges are not. Times of crisis and the disruptions they cause offer a unique lens through which to see the relationship between the material and non-material, the interrelation between the social and economic, and the innovative capacity of society. Examining how social entrepreneurs respond to disruption from crisis gives us insight into the interrelations between people and the spaces where values and social processes emerge.

We believe that understanding how social entrepreneurs responded to the pandemic will help us further unlock the ways in which they can support the global efforts to tackle grand challenges. Social entrepreneurs are uniquely placed due to their social embeddedness and strive for innovation. However, they also operate within established systems that are often resistant to change or are, at least, inert. The interlinked nature of grand challenges and wicked problems requires us to dive much deeper into the role of social entrepreneurs within systems change. Specifically, how factors that have so far only scarcely been addressed, such as space and the imaginary, enable or hinder the potential impact of social entrepreneurship on meeting grand challenges.

References

Barberá-Tomás, D., Castelló, I., De Bakker, F. G., & Zietsma, C. (2019). Energizing through visuals: How social entrepreneurs use emotion-symbolic work for social change. *Academy of Management Journal, 62*(6), 1789–1817.

Branzei, O., Parker, S. C., Moroz, P. W., & Gamble, E. (2018). Going pro-social: Extending the individual-venture nexus to the collective level. *Journal of Business Venturing, 33*(5), 551–565.

Castoriadis, C. (1977). The French Left. *Telos, 1977*(34), 49–73.

Castoriadis, C. (1987). *The imaginary institution of society*. Mit Press.

Castoriadis, C. (1992). Logic, imagination, reflection. *American Imago, 49*(1), 3–33.

Chamlee-Wright, E. (2007). The long road back: Signal noise in the post-Katrina context. *The Independent Review, 12*(2), 235–259.

Chamlee-Wright, E., & Storr, V. H. (2009). Club Goods and post-disaster community return, with Virgil Storr. *Rationality & Society, 21*(4), 429–458.

Chamlee-Wright, E., & Storr, V. H. (2010). The role of social entrepreneurship in post-Katrina community recovery. *International Journal of Innovation and Regional Development, 2*(1–2), 149–164.

Chamlee-Wright, E., & Storr, V. H. (2014). Commercial relationships and spaces after disaster. *Society, 51*(6), 656–664.

Corner, P. D., & Ho, M. (2010). How opportunities develop in social entrepreneurship. *Entrepreneurship Theory and Practice, 34*(4), 635–659.

Dacin, M. T., Dacin, P. A., & Tracey, P. (2011). Social entrepreneurship: A critique and future directions. *Organization Science, 22*(5), 1203–1213.

Dahl, M. S., & Sorenson, O. (2012). Home sweet home: Entrepreneurs' location choices and the performance of their ventures. *Management Science, 58*, 1227.

Datta, P. B., & Gailey, R. (2012). Empowering women through social entrepreneurship: Case study of a women's cooperative in India. *Entrepreneurship Theory and Practice, 36*(3), 569–587.

Dees, J. G. (1998). *The meaning of social entrepreneurship* (pp. 1–6). Fuqua School of Business Dukes University.

Dees, J. G. (2012). A tale of two cultures: Charity, problem solving, and the future of social entrepreneurship. *Journal of Business Ethics, 111*(3), 321–334.

Dees, J. G., & Anderson, B. B. (2006). Framing a theory of social entrepreneurship: Building on two schools of practice and thought. *Research on Social Entrepreneurship: Understanding and Contributing to an Emerging Field, 1*(3), 39–66.

Drucker, P. (1985). *Innovation and entrepreneurship: Practice and principles*. Harper & Row.

Drucker, P. (2012). *The frontiers of management*. Routledge.

Dutta, S. (2017). Creating in the crucibles of nature's fury: Associational diversity and local social entrepreneurship after natural disasters in California, 1991–2010. *Administrative Science Quarterly, 62*(3), 443–483.
George, G., Howard-Grenville, J., Joshi, A., & Tihanyi, L. (2016). Understanding and tackling societal grand challenges through management research. *Academy of Management Journal, 59*(6), 1880–1895.
Haeffele, S., & Craig, A. W. (2020). Commercial social spaces in the post-disaster context. *Journal of Entrepreneurship and Public Policy, 9*, 303–317.
Haugh, H. M., & Talwar, A. (2016). Linking social entrepreneurship and social change: The mediating role of empowerment. *Journal of Business Ethics, 133*(4), 643–658.
Hietschold, N., Voegtlin, C., Scherer, A. G., & Gehman, J. (2019). What we know and don't know about social innovation: A multi-level review and research agenda. In *Academy of management proceedings* (p. 12332). Academy of Management.
Hockerts, K. (2017). Determinants of social entrepreneurial intentions. *Entrepreneurship Theory and Practice, 41*(1), 105–130.
Ibrahim, S. E., & El Ebrashi, R. (2017). How social entrepreneurship can be useful in long-term recovery following disasters. *Journal of Humanitarian Logistics and Supply Chain Management, 7*, 324–349.
Mill, J. S. (1848). *Principles of political economy: With some of their applications to social philosophy* (Vol. 1).
Moerschell, L., & Novak, S. S. (2020). Managing crisis in a university setting: The challenge of alignment. *Journal of Contingencies and Crisis Management, 28*(1), 30–40.
Nicholls, A. (Ed.). (2008). *Social entrepreneurship: New models of sustainable social change*. OUP Oxford.
Nicholls, A. (2009). Learning to walk: Social entrepreneurship—A research review. In *Innovations* (pp. 209–222). Special Edition, Social Entrepreneurship
Nicholls, A., Simon, J., & Gabriel, M. (2015). *New frontiers in social innovation research*. Springer Nature.
Oldenburg, F. (2011). Social Entrepreneurship: Ein politisches Programm zur Innovationsförderung im Sozialsektor. In *Social entrepreneurship* (pp. 155–160). VS Verlag für Sozialwissenschaften.
Patalano, R. (2007). "Imagination and society. The affective side of institutions". *Constitutional Political Economy, 18*(4), 223–241.
Rushton, N. S. (2001). Monastic charitable provision in Tudor England: quantifying and qualifying poor relief in the early sixteenth century. *Continuity and Change, 16*(1), 9–44.
Santos, F., Pache, A. C., & Birkholz, C. (2015). Making hybrids work: Aligning business models and organizational design for social enterprises. *California Management Review, 57*(3), 36–58.

Say, J. B. (1846). *Traité d'économie politique: ou simple exposition de la manière dont se forment, se distribuent et se consomment les richesses* (Vol. 9). Guillaumin.

Schumpeter, J. A. (1939). *Business cycles* (Vol. 1, pp. 161–174). McGraw-Hill.

Schumpeter, J. A. (1947). The creative response in economic history. *The Journal of Economic History, 7*(2), 149–159.

Seelos, C., Mair, J., Battilana, J., & Dacin, M. T. (2011). The embeddedness of social entrepreneurship: Understanding variation across local communities. In *Communities and organizations*. Emerald Group Publishing Limited.

Shaw, E., & Carter, S. (2007). Social entrepreneurship: Theoretical antecedents and empirical analysis of entrepreneurial processes and outcomes. *Journal of Small Business and Enterprise Development, 14*(3), 418–434.

Shrivastava, P. (1993). Crisis theory/practice: Towards a sustainable future. *Industrial & Environmental Crisis Quarterly, 7*(1), 23–42.

Smith, A. (1776). *An inquiry into the nature and the causes of the wealth of nations. The Glasgow edition of the works and correspondence of Adam Smith. Reprint 20.* Palgrave Macmillan. https://doi.org/10.1057/9780230291652

Soros, G. (2000). *Open society; reforming global capitalism.* Public Affairs Press.

Stephan, U., Uhlaner, L. M., & Stride, C. (2015). Institutions and social entrepreneurship: The role of institutional voids, institutional support, and institutional configurations. *Journal of International Business Studies, 46*(3), 308–331.

Storr, V. H., Haeffele-Balch, S., & Grube, L. E. (2015). *Community revival in the wake of disaster: Lessons in local entrepreneurship*. Springer.

Storr, V. H., Haeffele-Balch, S., & Grube, L. E. (2017). Social capital and social learning after Hurricane Sandy. *The Review of Austrian Economics, 30*(4), 447–467.

Thompson, J., & Doherty, B. (2006). The diverse world of social enterprise: A collection of social enterprise stories. *International Journal of Social Economics, 33*, 361–375.

Wright, A. L., Meyer, A. D., Reay, T., & Staggs, J. (2020). Maintaining places of social inclusion: Ebola and the emergency department. *Administrative Science Quarterly*. https://doi.org/10.1177/0001839220916401

Yu, X. (2016). Social entrepreneurship in China's non-profit sector. The case of innovative participation of civil society in post-disaster reconstruction. *China Perspectives, 2016*(3), 53–61.

Zeyen, A., & Beckmann, M. (2018). *Social entrepreneurship and business ethics: Understanding the contribution and normative ambivalence of purpose-driven venturing*. Routledge.

Zeyen, A., Beckmann, M., & Akhavan, R. (2014). Social entrepreneurship business models: Managing innovation for social and economic value creation. In *Managementperspektiven für die Zivilgesellschaft des 21. Jahrhunderts* (pp. 107–132). Springer Gabler.

Zeyen, A., Beckmann, M., Mueller, S., Dees, J. G., Khanin, D., Krueger, N., Murphy, P. J., Santos, F., Scarlata, M., Walske, J. M., & Zacharakis, A. (2013). Social entrepreneurship and broader theories: Shedding new light on the 'Bigger Picture'. *Journal of Social Entrepreneurship, 4*(1), 88–107.

CHAPTER 3

Social Systems and Modern Society

Abstract Meeting the grand challenges and wicked problems of our time requires an in-depth understand of how the systems of society emerge and evolved into the modern society. This chapter introduces a systems lens, specifically a Luhmannian view of systems to understand grand challenges differently and examine the role of social entrepreneurship in initiating systems change. Seen through Lohmann's sociological perspective, we argue that wicked problems arise due to the challenges of communication across the social systems of modern society. Through this Luhmannian view, this chapter seeks to discuss why society is complex, how changes in one subsystem leads to adaptations in others, and briefly introduce the role of humans in the modern society.

Keywords Systems theory • Social systems • Action theory • Communication • Autopoiesis • Institutions

There are many, many, many worlds branching out at each moment you become aware of your environment and then make a choice
—Kevin Michel

E. Costales, A. Zeyen, *Social Entrepreneurship and Grand Challenges*, https://doi.org/10.1007/978-3-031-07450-9_3

3.1 A Brief History of Society

As we seek to navigate wicked problems, grand challenges, and the role social entrepreneurship plays in addressing them, we first have to examine the historical trajectories that have led us to where we are now. As mentioned in the previous chapters, addressing wicked problems and achieving grand challenges requires changing individual and societal behavior. Therefore, the central focus of this chapter revolves around the societal conditions which foster, restrain, and promote cooperation. The concept of institutions and institutional theory (Castoriadis, 1987; DiMaggio & Powell, 1983; North, 1990) as a guiding force for cooperation within society has been well received, and is something we advocate for throughout the book.

If institutions are the rules of the game in society, defined as "the humanly devised constraints that shape human interaction" (North, 1990, p. 3), then understanding institutions and institutional change requires us to examine the societal underpinnings which promote these humanly devised constraints. Friedrich Hayek offers an evolutionary trajectory of science and society in *The Counter Revolution of Science Studies on the Abuse of Reason* (1979) and *The Fateful Conceit: The Errors of Socialism* (1988). In these works, Hayek points to the idea that society and social order emerged from an unintentional adherence to moral practices (Hayek, 1988). Hayek suggests that the inability to perceive the validity of these practices through the senses does not diminish their validity and has led to the growth of population and wealth through their continued adoption. That is, the fact that people perceive different things similarly despite no known relation between them is the fundamental starting point for examining human behavior (Hayek, 1979).

As such, Hayek offers two forms of society: micro-cosmos and macro-cosmos, the latter of which are the building blocks of modern society. The micro-cosmos refers to small-group memberships which constituted early civilization. For example, anthropological nomadic tribes, early modern villages, or modern-day family structures are micro-cosmos. The micro-cosmos is characterized by intimate social interaction. Coordination within these groups depends on solidarity and altruism, which Hayek refers to as natural morality. Put differently, relationships in microcosms work because people know each other well and, importantly, are mutually dependent on one another.

On the other hand, the macro-cosmos refers to large group memberships which constitute modern society outside of families, neighborhoods, or local or religious communities. The macro-cosmos is characterized by impersonal and often anonymous social interaction (Hayek, 1988). Coordination within the macro-cosmos depend on rules which ensure cooperation between individuals who do not know one another. For example, buying a coffee at a coffee shop is, in many cases, an anonymous interaction. This is different to a microcosm as most interactions are less dependent on the individual's morals, i.e. the barrister does not first enquire about someone's values and beliefs before brewing a coffee for them. This form of interaction enables structures that emerged as part of modern society.

We belong to various micro-cosmos and macro-cosmos simultaneously, which forms the complex interrelations that give rise to wicked problems. In his 1993 work *Political Liberalism*, John Rawls builds on this Hayekian notion of dual cosmos and notes that pluralism has become a fact of modern society due to the variation in values and beliefs across society. The convergence of contrasting natural moralities from various micro-cosmos as they come in contract with one another initiates movement towards the macro-cosmos and necessitates the formation of rules to mitigate 'immoral' behavior; that is, behavior that contrasts with the natural morality of any given micro-cosmos. The expansion to the macro-cosmos has shifted society away from homogeneity to the point where universal consensus on conceptions of good or bad is no longer possible. Rawls refers to this as moral pluralism (Rawls, 1993), which we conjecture emerges from the duality of the cosmos. As we seek to balance solidarity, altruism, anonymity, and cooperation, people draw on various belief systems to direct their behavior towards cooperation (c.f. Galston, 2002). Let us take the United States political context as an example of this plurality of the cosmos. The United States constitution separates the church and the state, yet political discourse often centers around issues of religious sentiment. How is this so, given the separation of church and state? In the macro-cosmos (a citizen of the United States) there are formally codified rules (the constitution) which lay out rules of participating in the political process (separation of church and state). At the same time, however, there are the underpinnings of the micro-cosmos at play: the two-party system and the notion of solidarity to one's political party (e.g. Scholz, 2008). In a democratic society, the will of the majority is at play. If the micro-cosmos of the voters promotes objectives of religious-based solidarity, then the rules of the macro-cosmos (separation of church and state) are effectively subverted. In short, while political discourse should not be based on religion, individual pursuit of religious-based morality means that religion, while not explicitly, is not fully separated from the political realm.

Accounting for this plurality, we can conceptualize wicked problems as manifestations of tension between the various cosmos and the beliefs upon which they stand, where grand challenges represent the ideal reconciliations of these tensions. For example, SDG 16 (Peace and Justice) is a normative end condition most people can agree on—peace and justice is (usually) desirable. However, rules of the macro-cosmos (let us say the judicial system) may not adequately capture notions of peace and justice in the micro-cosmos. Take the use of cannabis in the United States or the United Kingdom vs. its decriminalization in the Netherlands. In the former context, the use of cannabis may constitute a criminal offense. Would this criminal offense be justice? It depends on who you ask—some groups may say yes, some may say no. Similarly, within the Netherlands, use of cannabis may not be a criminal offense, but should it? Again, it depends on who you ask—some groups may say yes, the others may say no. In short, what constitutes justice is a function of group solidarity: people who use cannabis are less likely to think of cannabis use as a criminal offense and far less likely to see fines or arrests as justice. Achieving the normative end conditions of grand challenges requires societal structures which enable reconciliation of tensions between the various cosmos to ensure cooperation. Thus, tackling wicked problems and achieving grand challenges first requires an understanding of the emergence and behavior of the systems of society.

3.2 What is the System?

When most people talk about the system it is usually in the context of change and at a surface level. "The system needs to be fixed", "it's the system's fault", or "fight the system" are the types of things we often hear when the system is mentioned. Even political discourses of 'the system' do not dive into the nuances of society's systems. Colloquially, a system can be understood as a set of interacting or interrelated entities that form a whole. But what does this mean? How do systems emerge and change? And how does understanding the system enable us, as a society, to reconcile the conflicts of the Hayekian cosmos?

There are multiple understandings of a system (e.g. Buckley, 1967; Giddens, 1979; Luhmann, 1986) with various attempts to present a theory of social systems (e.g. Brown, 1972; Parsons, 1951). Out of these multiple attempts emerged a competition between systems theory and action theory (Luhmann, 2013). Action theory, premised on structural functionalism (Parsons, 1951) encourages the analysis of structures which promulgate a social system. This analysis views a system as a technical instrument intended to rationalize and improve the structures of society. Indeed, systems were traditionally viewed as a summation of interrelated structures and processes (Bertalanffy, 1969). As such, action is presented as the unit of analysis for producing a system (e.g. Giddens, 1979; Parsons, 1951; Weber, 1985).

A general theory of systems requires recognition of the possibility for structures within a system to change without a dissolution of the system (Buckley, 1967). Thus, continuity of the system is vital to the system and developing a theory of the social system. Building off the theory of action, modern systems theories which seek to link action and structure as mutually constitutive elements of social systems have emerged. Structuration theory, promoted by Anthony Giddens, and Morphogenesis, promoted by Margaret Archer, are prominent among these theories. Morphogenesis and structuration align on the notion that social practices are shaped by unseen conditions of action, which generate unintended consequences, which in turn shape the context for future interaction (Archer, 2010). Their most prominent differences can be attributed to what can be called their end-states. In particular, structuration theory "ends" as a pattern of social practices which provide action and structure with new meaning (Giddens, 1979, 1980). By contrast, Morphogenesis "ends" with a concept known as structural elaboration, whereby the emerging structures have properties irreducible to the social practices which led to its emergence (Archer, 1995).

The German sociologist Niklas Luhmann takes a different approach to systems theory. Departing from action theory, Luhmann presents social systems as systems of communication, with society being the most encompassing social system (Luhmann, 1986). Building off the Parsonian notion that a society cannot exist other than as a system, Luhmann's theory is an abstract incorporation of action and systems theories which allows for more nuanced depictions of micro, meso, and macro structures. Moving away from functionalist interpretations of the system, Luhmann's theory views systems as self-reproducing through their own existence and as operationally closed to account for modern societal conditions and allow for structural change without dissolution of the system. For example, the dual cosmos of modern society means that the permissible actions for a given actor within society are bounded and shaped by available means in addition to varying social conditions. As Luhmann puts it, "a society is always already integrated either morally or by means of values or normative symbols before anyone can act in it" (Luhmann, 2013, p. 9). To Luhmann, society is comprised of linkages between biological, psychic, and social systems. The openness (or closure) of a system is thus contingent on conditioned relationships between these systems. In short, Luhmann only considers a "system" by its autopoietic operationalization. All else refers to the system's environment, irrespective of the role it plays in the system's continuity.

3.2.1 Luhmann's Autopoietic Social System

Fundamental to Luhmann's systems theory are the concepts of autopoiesis and communication (Luhmann, 1986). Luhmann incorporates and combines Maturana and Varela's (1980) notion of biological autopoietic materialism with Parson's (1951) theory of sociology to introduce his concept of the autopoietic social system. Autopoiesis holds that all elements of the system are produced through internal processes. That is, autopoietic systems are operatively closed. At the same time, they are interactionally open. While the operations of the autopoietic system cannot be produced externally, all autopoietic systems need to come into contact with their environments. Contact with the environment may lead to what Maturana and Varela (1980) refer to as perturbations: events external to the system which may trigger internal processes, but cannot determine them (Luhmann, 2000). The system's operative closure means that the system regulates exchanges with the environment and any internal process that may stem from perturbations. Thus, unlike the theories of structural functionalism, a system's structures are not pre-ordained as a consequence of historical human activity, but rather as the result of this process of autopoiesis. As the system reproduces itself, it self-organizes into structures which enable the autopoietic system's reproduction.

Given the simultaneous openness and closure of the autopoietic system, how does Luhmann incorporate the role of the environment? As mentioned above, a system's environment may trigger internal processes, but the outcome of these triggers are largely dependent on a system's structures. In short, a system's structures depend on its structural coupling with its environment. Structural coupling refers to a system's adaptability to structures in its environment, which prime its response to perturbations from the environment in question. Importantly, the societal system is divided into subsystems where each subsystem has all other subsystems in its environment. Moreover, humans are also situated in a system's environment. To fully understand the role of the environment, we need to step back and examine what the environment is.

Luhmann's autopoietic social system emphasizes the irreducibility of the social to biological, psychological, and cultural phenomena (Luhmann, 1986). He notes that the social realm relies on elements of biological functionalism, but they cannot be reduced to the biological level. Luhmann presents humans, and human behavior, as a union of biological and psychic systems which are interrelated with the social through structural coupling of the biological system structures—eyes and ears—and psychic system structures: cognition (Luhmann, 1986; Maturana & Varela, 1980). As autopoietic systems, biological systems and psychic systems are operatively closed, but they are structurally coupled to the extent that they allow for mutual perturbations. He notes that humans are necessary conditions for the continuity—and thus formation—of social systems, but are separate from them. Figure 3.1 provides an overview of the autopoietic systems within Luhmann's systems theory and their relation to one another.

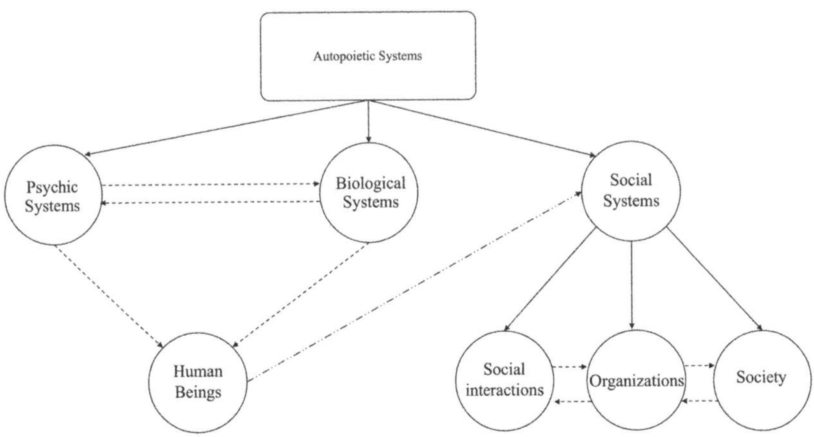

Fig. 3.1 Autopoietic systems within Luhmann's systems theory

3.2.2 *Luhmann and Communication*

There are three autopoietic systems in Luhmann's theory of social systems: biological systems, psychic systems, and social systems. The dashed arrows in Fig. 3.1 indicate directionality of structural coupling, bearing in mind that structural coupling can only take place between two systems which is at any given point a system and its environment. The differently dashed arrow between human beings and social systems illustrates the necessity of human beings for the emergence of social systems. Social systems are further broken down into society, organizations, and social interactions. Luhmann argues, in contrast to action theory, that the social dimension is brought into reality through communication as the fundamental unit—not action. The psychic system is necessary for communication, and while the same is true for action, Luhmann argues that action can be a solitary behavior and thus does not generate its own continuity. Communication, in contrast, is a system-producing operation because it requires social contexts to emerge, thereby forming the boundary of a social system (Luhmann, 2018).

Luhmann defines communication as the synthesis of utterance, information, and understanding. That is, the synthesis of the method through which something is conveyed, the information conveyed, and the processing of the information from the receiver. For Luhmann, the method through which something is conveyed is not limited to any particular language or action. The implications are that communication is vital for the existence of social systems, and communication maintains an element of subjectivity whereby it is shaped by the receiver rather than the deliverer. Let us take Luhmann's example of looking at a watch during a social interaction. Person A and person B are having a conversation, and person A looks at their watch. Looking at their watch constitutes an utterance. Within this utterance is (at least) two pieces of information: (i) person A is checking the time, or (ii) person A is bored of the conversation. At this juncture, the outcome of the social interaction sits with person B. Communication is 'complete' when person B processes the available information as either (i) or (ii). As we can imagine, processing the information as (i) or (ii) may be the difference between offense and conflict or pleasant and peaceful. If person B processes the information as (ii) and this was not person A's intention, then any potential conflict may be mediated by a subsequent social interaction whereby person A says sorry or explains. Each of these mediating attempts are utterances (talking) and the method of talking makes the information more easily processable by person B. As mentioned above, humans are unions of autopoietic systems, with the psychic system representing the cognition of meaning. Person A's psychic system and person B's psychic system represent environments to one another. There, the psychic system of person B can never enter the psychic system of person A. In short, person B cannot know what person A is thinking, only the utterances of person A. Thus, the social interaction between the two is an autopoietic social system based on the communications of meaning, whereby language emerges as a codifier which structures the perturbations of psychic systems during this process of communication. As social interaction between person A and person B progresses over time, the social system (social interactions) develops expectations of perturbations from environments A and B through the codification of language. From Luhmann's perspective, people can be defined as complex expectations of perturbations from a unity of biological and psychic systems. For the social system (social interaction), communication of meaning is structured by a process of codification (in this case language) which is the result of recursive interactions of expectations, which are themselves the result of codes that resulted from interactions. In short, a social structure emerges in our watch example from an iterative process of codification (language) which aligns the utterance (looking at the watch), information (just checking the time), and understanding (process of checking the time instead of being bored). Figure 3.2 illustrates this social interaction, and language as a codifier emerging from recursive interactions.

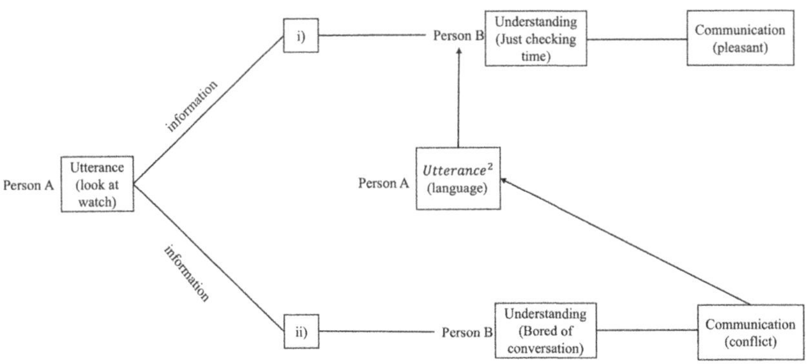

Fig. 3.2 Social interaction and emergence of language as structure for mediating communication

Communication becomes communication only through structural coupling which enables a communication to perturb a system to the extent that the information presented by the environment is acted upon through the internal processes of that system. Luhmann introduces the concept of interpenetration to refer to specific couplings of social and psychic systems to the extent one (or both) systems treat each other like parts of their own system (Luhmann, 2013). Returning to our watch example, the psychic systems of person A and person B can never be one with each other or the social system of their interaction. However, over time, the social system has developed expectations of environments A and B to the extent that A and B have interpenetrated the social system. That is, in the social interaction between person A and person B, the utterance of looking at a watch mid-conversation is an expected—and thus communicatively expedited—method of communicating an interest in the time rather than boredom.

At first glance this is a bland and somewhat confusing distinction, but upon inspection we see a cohesion of action theory and systems theory, previously thought to be incompatible (Leydesdorff, 1996; Luhmann, 1982, 2018). Autopoiesis of social systems emerges from the reproduction of communications among various systems and provides a path forward for examining the relation between the micro and macro cosmos and modern society. The iterative communication and structural emergence from our watch example can be extrapolated to the various autopoietic systems in Luhmann's theory.

3.3 Modern Society: A Luhmann Perspective

Luhmann conceptualizes society as the most encompassing social system. In fact, in his 1997 work *Globalization or World Society: How to conceive of modern society?*, Luhmann argues that the hierarchical differentiation of the past has been replaced with functional differentiation. Aligning with the Hayekian notion of the dual cosmos, he points out that the concept of solidarity which bounds collective consciousness of the micro-cosmos has since been replaced with societal plurality due to the advent of the macro-cosmos which functional differentiation has enabled. Functional differentiation in the modern context, refers to subsystems of society which include and exclude people through their functionalities (Luhmann, 1997). This process of subsystem emergence is due to what Luhmann refers to the differential theoretical approach (Luhmann, 2013). In short, the boundaries between a system and its environment form the basis for which a system generates its own continuity through its functional operations.

In keeping with the notion of autopoiesis, society distinguishes between itself, humans (the unity of biological and psychic systems), and ecological conditions which constitute the non-human environment. Structural coupling and interpenetration require language (codification) as a mechanism of communication. As mentioned in the previous section, humans are vital to reproducing systems and functional differentiation precisely because they are not part of society. The cognitive processes of the psychic system allow for structural coupling and expectation alterations which account for changes to social structures through functionally distinct instantiations. In short, while people may not be part of society, their communicative capacity make them vital for its continuity.

As mentioned above, the functionalities of modern society manifest through social systems which shape the macro-cosmos people belong to on the basis of their functionalities. In the macro-cosmos, functional differentiation of autopoietic social systems provide exclusive societal functions. For example, the economic system—in which all people participate—is the only thing that can communicate payment; only the political system can communicate authority; and only the judicial system can communicate justice. Each of these systems communicate through exhaustive binary function specific codes. The economic system encompasses all economic communication, with money as the medium of exchange; the judicial system encompasses all legal communication, with guilt as the medium of exchange; and the political system encompasses all political communication, with power as the medium of exchange.[1]

Following autopoiesis, the economic and judicial system reproduce internally and communicate with one another only as perturbations that invoke internal processes based on their own mediums of exchange. In short, the economic system communicates through a binary codification of pay/no pay, while the legal system communicates through a binary codification of guilty/not guilty, and the political system communicates as win/lose. They are structurally coupled to the extent that modern society operates through the systems' adjustment to one another's functions. Seidl (2004) uses the example of the sales contract to highlight this coupling. "The sales contract is two different communications for the two

[1] 'Money' in this case does not refer to fiat currency in the colloquial sense, but rather to any mechanism of exchange that communicates pay/not pay

different function systems [economic and judicial systems], but it allows the two systems to somewhat 'co-ordinate' their respective processes" (Seidl, 2004, p. 14). In the micro-cosmos, the social systems of which we are part operate on the same autopoietic foundations. The familiarity of the micro-cosmos, however, means that the functional differentiation of social systems includes rather than exclude through their functionalities. The argument can then be made that the micro-cosmos preserves solidarity in a way that the macro-cosmos does not, thus, social systems at the micro-cosmos operate practically at a more person-centered level as a result of the solidarity or natural morality. For example, the economic system communicates through pay/no pay, which, due to structural coupling with the legal and political systems, requires currency.

3.3.1 Institutions in the Autopoietic Society

Given the basis of autopoiesis and the role and reflexivity of communication discussed above, how does this shape our understanding of our own roles in society? To recap, modern society is comprised of three autopoietic systems: biological systems, psychic systems, and social systems. Social systems form the dual cosmos we all belong to and can be further broken down into society, organizations, and social interactions. The autopoiesis of society, as a macro-cosmos, replicates itself on the basis of functional differentiation premised on the societal functions they serve (such as economic, justice, political, or scientific). Structures form within these systems based on expectations of perturbations from communicating with their environments (including each other and people) and can adapt to one another to the point that they respond to one another as if they were one. The autopoiesis of social interactions as a micro-cosmos replicates itself on intimate relations between psychic systems whose communications are replicated on the basis of solidarity or natural morality. Organizations can be seen as mediators between the two and they replicate on the basis of decisions as a specific form of communication.

The concept of functional differentiation and operative closure may seem, at first, to suggest that humans do not have much agency in relation to system behavior. Humans are on one hand a necessary unit for the formation of social systems, and on the other hand they are not part of society. This seemingly paradoxical positionality of the human being is the foundation of wicked problems and grand challenges. Returning to the propositions from Chap. 1, we argue that wicked problems persist because they are unclear and loosely defined by self-referential and autopoietic systems. Given the nature of autopoiesis as described above, the relation between grand challenges, wicked problems, and social entrepreneurship is more easily conceptualized. Grand challenges are the cognitive notions of the desired end conditions from the complex interplay of internally reproductive functional systems: they represent the *what*: what do we want to achieve? Wicked problems are the complex interplay between the autopoietic systems of modern society which obfuscate achieving our desired end conditions: they represent the *why*: why does current structural coupling (or lack thereof) between the subsystems overlook and promulgate certain issues? Social entrepreneurship is a tool for societal change and represents the *how*: how can humans encourage the structural coupling necessary for the causes of wicked problems to be recognized by the system and achieve grand challenges?

As the only autopoietic system with cognition, humans hold the key for translating societal issues into recognizable perturbations to the extent that the functional systems of society develop structures and begin to adapt to wicked problems. In order to understand how social entrepreneurship might encourage the structural coupling, we first need to examine how humans interact with one another. As mentioned in Sect. 3.3.1, institutions have emerged and taken center stage as an explanatory guiding force for human behavior. Extant literature has demonstrated that institutional change is necessary to promote change at the level of social interaction (e.g. Beckmann, 2011; Pies et al., 2009, 2010). History has demonstrated the importance of institutions ranging back as far as the sixteenth century (North, 1990). Institutions are the humanly devised and socially sanctioned constraints that shape human interaction and maintain functional (North, 1991) and symbolic (Castoriadis, 1987) components. They may be informal (such as customs or other social norms of solidarity and altruism, seen in the micro-cosmos) or formal (such as codified laws put in place to maintain cooperation in the anonymity of the macro-cosmos) and they serve to maintain a sense of order and significance in socio-economic life (DiMaggio & Powell, 1991; North, 1990). While the economic functionality of institutions aligns with Luhmann's concept of functional differentiation, the role of human behavior in the autopoietic society requires recognition of the cognitive capacity of human beings extending beyond the economic system.

Borrowing from institutional analysis (Castoriadis, 1977) we return to the social imaginary from Chap. 2 and insert it into the autopoietic society to incorporate a 'beyond functionalist' view of institutions. The radical imaginary captures the structural coupling between the biological and psychic systems which make up the human being. It accounts for the interplay between the biological systems (eyes, ears, body) and the psychic system (cognition) in developing rules of interaction that extend beyond economic functionality and incorporate symbolism drawn from individual persons' perception of their environment. Such symbolism accounts for the evolution of rules from the natural moralities of the micro-cosmos to the functional rules of the macro-cosmos (c.f. Hayek, 1988). The social imaginary captures the communicative link between human beings and the social systems which make up their environments, and the ability to impart meaning beyond what can be empirically proven (Castoriadis, 1987; Patalano, 2007; Weber, 1985).

Autopoietic systems have communication of meaning as the mechanisms of self-referential reproduction, and meanings are simultaneously subject and society dependent; they manifest only through the cognitive systems of people, who are themselves embedded within a social context. Thus, new meanings emerge in tension with existing mental structures (Bouilloud et al., 2020) and are actualized by repeated communication, which becomes socialized through a socio-symbolic acceptance of social interactions over time. If we refer to our previous watch example, social acceptance of looking at a watch during a conversation emerges over time as the meaning associated with looking at the watch moves away from 'bored' and towards 'checking the time'. Traditionally, such communication has been viewed as a function of individual economic and psychological investments (c.f. North, 1991). The concept of crystallized mental models and motivations suggests that when an opportunity leads to a successful investment (communicative behavior), perception of this investment (communicative behavior) may transform into a belief, which forms a positive emotion and incentivizes future communication (action). When a similar opportunity arises, the positive emotion forms the motivation for a repeated communicative behavior (Mantzavinos et al., 2004).

In the autopoietic society, the premise of the communication of value as the fundamental unit requires a wide scope for capturing the meaning making process. The notion of crystallized mental models and subsequent motivations anchors the meaning making process within an economic construct (Vouldis, 2018), which is too narrow for fully capturing the communication of meaning and value. While we do not disagree with the functional aspect of institutions, we argue that functionalism and neo-institutionalism overlooks significant symbolic elements which give rise to agentic potential of humans to influence institutional change. For example, though markets are efficient stewards for the institution of capitalism, within the economic system, and the second-order institution of a business within the organization social system, markets are significantly less efficient at measuring and promoting equality. Indeed, social value often exists at a level which is not translatable in the codification of the traditional market. As a structure within the economic system, the medium of exchange within the market is pay/no pay. However, a good or service which provides a social value may not be affordable and thus the 'no pay' communication is received by the market despite the good or service's potential desirability from a sustainability standpoint. The combination of castoridian institutional analysis (Castoriadis, 1987) and functional institutional analysis (DiMaggio & Powell, 1983; North, 1990) enables us to analyze the ways in which human actors can navigate the autopoietic society to look beyond institutional functionalism and incorporate the communicative capacity of individuals to influence symbolic characteristics of change. As individuals' environments change, it perturbs the psychic system and initiates meaning-making, which is institutionalized through prolonged social interaction to the extent they interpenetrate society and its subsystems. This interpenetration induces structural change through repeated communication of new meaning between functional systems and their respective functions.

Despite not being part of society, humans have the potential to alter system structures by conditioning expectations of their own perturbations to social systems through institutional constraints. In short, changing themselves (how they irritate a given system) can lead to the system changing itself through repeated communication of new meaning which, over time, leads to interpenetration. This reversal of agency, as it were, and emphasis on the role of communication may hold the key to unlocking the barriers to grand challenges and present a pathway for addressing wicked problems via institutional change that initiates widespread structural coupling and interpenetration to the extent that cognitive end conditions for society can be achieved. The following chapter builds on Luhmann's society to examine how individuals—specifically social entrepreneurs—navigate and create disruption as a method of communication to influence the change necessary to meet our cognitive end conditions.

References

Archer, M. S. (1995). *Realist social theory: The morphogenetic approach.* Cambridge University Press.

Archer, M. S. (2010). Morphogenesis versus structuration: on combining structure and action. *The British Journal of Sociology, 61,* 225–252.

Beckmann, M. (2011). The social case as a business case: Making sense of social entrepreneurship from an ordonomic perspective. In *Corporate citizenship and new governance* (pp. 91–115). Springer.

Bertalanffy, L. V. (1969). *General system theory: Foundations, development, applications.* George Braziller.

Bouilloud, J. P., Perezts, M., Viale, T., & Schaepelynck, V. (2020). Beyond the stable image of institutions: Using institutional analysis to tackle classic questions in institutional theory. *Organization Studies, 41*(2), 153–174.

Brown, S. G. (1972). *Laws of form.* The Library of Science Bookclub.

Buckley, W. (1967). Sociology and modern systems theory.

Castoriadis, C. (1977). The French Left. *Telos, 1977*(34), 49–73.

Castoriadis, C. (1987). *The imaginary institution of society.* Mit Press.

DiMaggio, P. J., & Powell, W. W. (1983). The Iron Cage Revisited: Institutional Isomorphism and Collective Rationality in Organizational Fields. *American Sociological Review, 48*(2), 147–160. https://doi.org/10.2307/2095101

DiMaggio, P. J., & Powell, W. W. (1991). Introduction to the new institutionalism. The new institutionalism in organizational analysis, 1–38.

Galston, W. A. (2002). *Liberal pluralism: The implications of value pluralism for political theory and practice.* Cambridge University Press.

Giddens, A. (1979). *Central problems in social theory: Action, structure, and contradiction in social analysis* (Vol. 241). University of California Press.

Giddens, A. (1980). *Classes, capitalism, and the state.* Springer.

Hayek, F. A. (1979). *The counter-revolution of science: Studies on the abuse of reason.* Liberty Press.

Hayek, F. A. (1988). *The fatal conceit: The errors of socialism* (W. W. Bartley, Ed.). University of Chicago Press.

Leydesdorff, L. (1996). Luhmann's sociological theory: its operationalization and future perspectives. *Social Science Information, 35*(2), 283–306.

Luhmann, N. (1982). The world society as a social system. *Int. J. General Systems 8*, 131–138.

Luhmann, N. (1986). *Love as passion: The codification of intimacy.* Harvard University Press.

Luhmann, N. (1997). Globalization or world society: how to conceive of modern society? *International Review of Sociology, 7*(1), 67–79.

Luhmann, N. (2000). Organisation und Entscheidung. Opladen: Westdeutscher Verlag.

Luhmann, N. (2013). *Introduction to systems theory* (D. Baecker, Ed., P. Gilgen, Trans. from German). Polity.

Luhmann, N. (2018). *Organization and Decision* (D. Baecker, Ed., R. Barrett, Trans. from German). Cambridge University Press.

Mantzavinos, C., North, D. C., & Shariq, S. (2004). Learning, institutions, and economic performance. *Perspectives on Politics, 2*, 75–84.

Maturana, H., & Varela, F. (1980). *Autopoiesis and cognition: The realization of the living*. Reidel.

North, D. C. (1990). *Institutions, institutional change and economic performance*. Cambridge University Press.

North, D. C. (1991). Institutions. *Journal of Economic Perspectives, 5*(1), 97–112.

Parsons, T. (1951). *The social system*. Psychology Press.

Patalano, R. (2007). "Imagination and society". *The affective side of institutions. Constitutional Political Economy, 18*(4), 223–241.

Pies, I., Hielscher, S., & Beckmann, M. (2009). Moral commitments and the societal role of business: An ordonomic approach to corporate citizenship. *Business Ethics Quarterly, 19*(3), 375–401.

Pies, I., Beckmann, M., & Hielscher, S. (2010). Value creation, management competencies, and global corporate citizenship: An ordonomic approach to business ethics in the age of globalization. *Journal of Business Ethics, 94*(2), 265–278.

Rawls, J. (1993). *Political liberalism*. Columbia University Press.

Scholz, S. J. (2008). *Political solidarity*. Penn State Press.

Seidl, D. (2004). Luhmann's theory of autopoietic social systems. *Munich Business Research, 2*, 1–28.

Vouldis, A. T. (2018). Cornelius Castoriadis on institutions: a proposal for a schema of institutional change. *Cambridge Journal of Economics, 42*(5), 1435–1458.

Weber, M. (1985). *Gesammelte Aufsätze zur Wissenschaftslehre*. Hrsg. von Johannes Winckelmann. 6., erneut durchgesehene Auflage, Tübingen: J. C. B. Mohr (Paul Siebeck) (1. Auflage 1922)

CHAPTER 4

Spaces and Places from the Imagination to Reality: The Case of the Global COVID-19 Spatial Lockdowns

Abstract The concept of the radical imaginary is a vital element for incorporating the human capacity to impart meaning and value on various objects. Socializing this imaginary is a vital process for meeting grand challenges in the autopoietic society. In this chapter, we demonstrate the role of place as a practical manifestation of the social imaginary and space as a tool for rule-setting behavior, through a longitudinal case analysis which explores how social entrepreneurs responded to spatial disruption in light of the COVID-19 lockdowns. In doing so, we analyze which elements of space social entrepreneurs engage with to affect change. We induce the concept of sociomateriality to explore the extent to which the digital dimension of space is adopted as an intermediary through which space is (pre)constructed and enables social imaginaries to manifest in the physical realm. We further induce the concept of psychological distance to examine how space is used as a tool for communicating meaning through the construction of space. This chapter offers an overview of the Netnographic and practice tracing methodologies for future researchers interested in grand challenges.

E. Costales, A. Zeyen, *Social Entrepreneurship and Grand Challenges*, https://doi.org/10.1007/978-3-031-07450-9_4

Keywords Space • Place • Psychological distance • Social imaginary • COVID-19 • Netnography • Practice-tracing

Imagination does not become great until human beings, given the courage and the strength, use it to create
—Maria Montessori

4.1 What Do We Mean by Place and Space?

The complexities of place and space are best illustrated by the extent to which one is subsumed by the other. Place and space are often used interchangeably; however, the Oxford English Dictionary defines place as "a particular point or region of space", while space is defined as "the volume or dimensional extent that is, or may be, occupied by a particular thing". We make the distinction that place maintains particular and distinguishable material characteristics. This chapter adopts an analytically phenomenological view of place as a manifestation of economic and social processes in space, which involves distinctive adoption of and organization within space (Agnew, 2011). Space is therefore a phenomenal reality within which place is located, and it is the meaning-making processes of place that shapes the configuration of space. Place is bounded space within which meanings and the material converge (Gieryn, 2000). Articulating meaning through communication (including behavior) is fundamental to the development of place (Jones et al., 2019). In fact, communication with the material defines place and endows it with ever evolving meaning (Goldhagen & Gallo, 2017).

4.1.1 *The Opportunities of Space*

The materiality of space refers to constituent characteristics of space which are static from one moment to the next and available to all users in the same way (Leonardi, 2012); affordance scholars hold that these properties afford utility to be leveraged through individual agency (e.g., Gibson, 1986; Leonardi & Barley, 2010) such as the forming of collectives (c.f. Archer, 1995). Affordance refers to the potential activities enabled by these properties (e.g. Gibson, 1966; Norman, 1999). Blagoev et al. (2019) draw attention to the communicative and interactional potential of space. However, co-location per se is insufficient to encourage social engagement (Hampton & Gupta, 2008). Indeed, meaningful social engagement is a function of meaning and the social imaginary. Sociomateriality research holds that social and material elements of the physical world are mutually constitutive, whose interplay have significant implications for how social and economic processes are conducted (e.g. de Moura & Bispo, 2020; Orlikowski & Scott, 2008). We endorse Orlikowski's (2007, p. 1438) definition of sociomateriality as "the constitutive entanglement of the social and the material in everyday organizational life". At first glance, sociomateriality and affordances adopt contrasting perspectives regarding the role of human agency. That is, an affordance perspective puts forward that the material enables the actualization of human agency, while sociomateriality maintains a relational and mutually constitutive view. It is not the purpose of this chapter to advocate one perspective; rather we borrow from both perspectives to account for the role of pre-existing entrenched social structures in shaping how spatial configurations emerge. To this effect, we incorporate sociomateriality as a basis for affordances, whereby the relationality of space expresses itself through the affordances provided by spatial configurations and sensitizes us to the role of the (non)material.

In fact, social and economic behaviors are often entangled; colleagues may become friends during work luncheons, friends may initiate economic ventures in a coffee shop, and charitable organizations may hold rallies at local businesses (e.g. Storr, 2009; Haeffele & Craig, 2020). Space has always played a constraining or supportive role in the context of organizational behavior (Lô & Diochon, 2019). Current scholarship has become fascinated with the material-social relationship and the extent to which entrepreneurs create such spaces intentionally versus ad hoc organizational reorientation towards community development across time (e.g. Haeffele & Craig, 2020; Goermar et al., 2020; Chamlee-wright & Storr, 2014; Bansal & Knox-hayes, 2013; Zeyen et al., 2014).

Extant literature examines the changing use and value of space by examining how traditional commercial and social space is co-opted for different purposes. In particular, research into 'Co-working spaces' (e.g. Bouncken & Reuschl, 2018; Tremblay & Scaillerez, 2020) and 'Third (work)spaces' (e.g. Bhabha, 1994; Kingma, 2016; Oldenburg, 1989) is key to the discussion. Through closing the distance between like-minded people, Co-working spaces such as WeWork, Betahaus, Accrue workplaces, and Plexel endeavor to reinject the social element of economic activity. Such spaces are membership-based shared work environments designed to provide necessary infrastructure and engender social ties (e.g. Bouncke & Reuschl, 2018; Spinuzzi, 2012). As such, coworking spaces represent platforms for community building and knowledge exchange (c.f. Ballon et al., 2015; Täuscher & Laudien, 2018) for independent workers—"[those] loosely connected to organizations or selling directly to the market" (Petriglieri et al., 2019, p. 125).

In contrast, the modern third space refers to hybrid work environments (e.g. Kingma, 2016) which are often places beyond the boundaries of home and the traditional workplace (Oldenburg, 1989). They invoke Bhabha's (1994) notion of the third space as a discursive space beyond walls, where culture and identity are constructed. The implication is that modern third spaces emerge—insomuch as they are a workspace, as a function of the economic processes which give rise to the construction of place and the meaning-making processes by which user(s) adopt this place as an area for constructing a work identity. That is, third spaces such as cafes, coffeshops, bars, or community centers (e.g. Lô & Diochon, 2019) emerge as a consequence of the economic processes by which commercial entities develop and the meaning-making processes of the user(s) by which these spaces transform into third spaces. The materiality of such places affords meaning-making processes due to their inclusivity, accessibility to the general public, and absence of membership or exclusion criteria (Oldenburg, 1989).

Though they do overlap, we must be careful not to conflate the modern third space with 'Social Spaces'. Indeed, the latter refers to virtual or physical spaces that enable interaction for community strength and (re) development (e.g. Chamlee-Wright & Storr, 2014). We draw a distinction here that it is social processes which are the primary forces giving rise to social spaces, in contrast to the economic processes which give rise to third spaces in the first instance and become designated as such through social processes. Principally, social spaces represent gathering places for existing collectivities, and provide opportunities for individuals to engage with new collectives (Haeffele & Craig, 2020). As such, their existence and appeal are considerably more susceptible to change in accordance to shifting social imaginaries.

We look to construal level theory (Liberman & Trope, 2008) to examine how space is used as a tool for communicating meaning by manifesting the social imaginary. Construal level theory posits that meaning-making, decisions, and subsequent behavior is a function of psychological distance (Trope & Liberman, 2010). Psychological distance refers to the perceived similarities between people. And elements of a given phenomenon (Liberman & Trope, 2008; Trope & Liberman, 2003, 2010). As this distance grows, so too does the level of abstraction with which someone engages with a social problem (c.f. Chen et al., 2018). Low level construal refers to concrete and contextual interpretations of objects or events, while high level construal involves abstract and decontextualized interpretations (Liberman & Trope, 2008). Spatial configurations affect psychological distance in three ways: (i) embedding values within material and social elements of place (e.g. Wright et al., 2020; de Moura & Bispo, 2020), (ii) contextualizing and actualizing embedded values through norms (Trope & Liberman, 2003), (iii) enhancing social interaction of diverse psychic systems (people) to promote goal alignment and management of psychological distance (Branzei et al., 2018; Powell et al., 2018).

People have a tendency to interpret situations nearer to them through a more practical lens, while they opt for a moral lens towards issuers that are distant to them (Eyal et al., 2008). Zeyen and Beckmann (2018) show that situations require reconciliation between moral normativity and situation specific considerations to determine which course of action should be taken. Indeed, the pluralistic society means that morality is insufficient for decisions within the dual-cosmos. Unchecked normativity can lead to normativistic fallacies and exacerbation of social ailments (see Zeyen & Beckmann, 2018). Too much emphasis on what should be done without consideration for practical realities gives rise to errors of the third kind and inhibit movement towards grand challenges (this is further examined in Chap. 6). Managing psychological distance has the potential to reduce such fallacies. As psychic systems are repeatedly perturbed by other psychic systems, the social interaction allows for the communication of respective cognitive responses to their individual environments. In short, contracting psychological distance stems from communicating lived experiences and situation specific considerations.

The complexity of wicked problems such as poverty (Acemoglu et al., 2001; Banerjee & Duflo, 2011), inequality (Sen, 1999), and inclusivity (Mair et al., 2012; Stephan et al., 2015; Yunus et al., 2010) highlights the value of others in goal setting, opportunity recognition, and creative problem-solving (Grant & Berry, 2011; Moulaert et al., 2013), which requires a mix of high- and low-level construal. Collective interpretation and meaning-making are vital for goal setting, at the collective level, to address wicked problems (André et al., 2018). Powell et al. (2018) point out that collective understanding has the potential to ameliorate impediments to cooperation that can arise from material conflicts and value asymmetries. The multiplicity of meanings imparted on place enables the management of construal levels to the extent they converge upon collective norms. We would then expect phenomena understood within a particular place to be addressed less abstractly. In other words, the boundlessness of space represents a higher level of construal with higher levels of abstraction (Trope & Liberman, 2010), while the bounded nature of place involves a lower level of abstraction where psychological distance can be pro- or contracted.

The boundary crossing capabilities of communicative technology is creating a world in which place and space begin to blur (e.g. Friedman, 2005) with significant implications for social and economic processes. The increased 'placelessness' emerging from widespread use of communicative technology mirrors an increasing trend of individualization of work (Goermar et al., 2020). 36% of American workers freelanced in 2021 (Ozimek, 2021) and, according to the Office of National Statistics, 12.5% of laborers in the UK identified as self-employed in 2019 (ONS, 2020). Similarly, communication technology enables employers to implement remote working models. Despite the ease of communication and perception of contracted distance emerging from the internet revolution (Goldenberg & Levy, 2009), many remote workers are left socially adrift and opt to conduct work in places such as coffee shops or libraries (Garrett et al., 2017). Motivation for working in locations such as coffee shops may stem from a desire to work near social activity unavailable at home or in the office (c.f. Oldenburg, 1989). In such instances, the materiality of place affords opportunity for social activity.

4.1.2 Space in Times of Disruption

Crisis brings the prosociality of place to the fore and highlights the plurality of spatial configurations and influence of social processes on the usage of place and space. While crises enable us to see the malleability of place and space by forcing us to examine the complexity of what is taken for granted, not all crises are equal. That is, the disruptions they cause may be quick and confined to specific areas of cartesian space (such as hurricanes, earthquakes, tornadoes, or floods) while others may be slow onset and encompass vast areas of space and time (such as droughts or wars). The COVID-19 crisis introduces unique spatial disruption and a once in a lifetime lens through which to analyze the relation between meaning and space. Disruption caused by COVID-19 is not constrained to any particular point within cartesian space, but rather encompasses all physical space. Similarly, in contrast to crises such as drought, earthquakes, or hurricanes, the post-crisis phase of COVID-19 requires creation and dissemination of a vaccine; actors cannot conduct activities at another physical point in cartesian space because the whole world was struck by COVID-19.

Governments around the world enacted social distancing and lockdown measures as part of their efforts to combat the virus. As a result, thousands of businesses were closed, millions of people lost their jobs, and the traditional role of space was significantly changed. As social distancing and digital interaction became the new norm, the world was forced to reassess the spatial dimension of economic and social activity, and the role of technology in this dynamic. As a society, the closest event we have to the COVID-19 pandemic in terms of scope and impact is the 1918 influenza pandemic. Over four waves, lasting 2 years, more than 20 million people lost their lives—more than 3 times the death toll from COVID-19 (c.f. Patterson & Pyle, 1991). Notwithstanding the medical advances made over the century, digitalization is the biggest distinction between these pandemics. Thus, the impacts of COVID-19 on modern society cannot be separated from the role of technology. In particular, how the digital dimension relates to physical space.

Much of the management literature using sociomateriality as a theoretical framework looks at the organizing potential of mixed-use and third spaces (e.g. Garrett et al., 2017), value creation within such spaces, the balance between formality and informality for leveraging organizational capacity, or the creation of non-commercial relations through commercial spaces, particularly in times of crisis (e.g. Chamlee-Wright & Storr, 2014; Haeffele & Craig, 2020). The uniqueness of COVID-19 allows us to analyze the innovative capacity of society emerging from the relationship between the material and non-material. This chapter analyses this innovative capacity through the lens of social entrepreneurs by examining how they respond to spatial constraints. In situations such as COVID-19 where traditional meaning making processes and utilization of place are upset, society must become more sensitive to, and engage with, the social imaginary, emergent endowments of meaning, and the extent to which social entrepreneurs engage with this new meaning.

We do this through a netnographic methodology with 17 social entrepreneurs in the Netherlands and the United Kingdom to examine how digital space enables (pre)construction of physical space. Following accepted practice for data collection in sociomateriality research (e.g. Fenwick et al., 2015) we also use a practice-tracing methodology (Pouliot, 2015) to examine the role of space in routine behavior, and the extent to which the digital dimension of space enables the physical manifestation of shared social imaginaries at multiple phases of the COVID-19 crisis. Social entrepreneurial engagement with space is delineated in terms of the social and material elements they utilize to meet their remit.

4.2 Netnography in COVID-19: A Brief Overview

Netnography adapts traditional ethnographic methods for studying emerging online communities (Kozinets, 2002, 2010) and is therefore apropos for following engagement with the digital dimension (e.g. Archibald et al., 2019), particularly given physical spatial constraints imposed by the enforcement of lockdown. Ethnography refers to a group of methods which involve direct and sustained contact with participants and recording the encounters to represent the experiences of the people under observation (Willis & Trondman, 2000). To collect our data, however, we adopted a critical realist ethnography (see Bhaskar, 1998) whereby we maintained consistent awareness that participants' interpretations of events represent one stratum of reality. We incorporate the stratified differentiation of distinctions between the domains of real, actual, and empirical. These refer to the structures that generate the world, events that occur regardless of perception, and what people perceive through their senses, respectively (see Leca & Naccache, 2006).

As part of our netnography, author 1 engaged with a digital platform which was the result of collaboration between two organizations aimed to promote youth impact entrepreneurship. In addition, author 1 participated in online events held through this shared digital space as well as those held by individual social entrepreneurs. To further substantiate our data, author 1 maintained periodic email correspondence with participants to check-in and receive bi-weekly updates. Furthermore, participants were given diaries and asked to log at least 10 entries over the ten months, in a semi-structured format. Following accepted practice, participants engaged in pre- and post-diary semi-structured interviews averaging 1 hour (Ohly et al., 2010; Wickham & Knee, 2013). As our data collection began prior to global social distancing measures, a practice-tracing methodology (Pouliot, 2015) allows us to determine points of inflection, whereby usage of space is affected by each phase of the COVID-19 crisis. This enables us to examine the convergence of shared meanings imparted in space and analyze the interplay between social and material elements of space. The combination provides a unique lens for examining the aspects of space which are most important for social entrepreneurs to meet their remits, by identifying which aspects are necessary for their practices.

With this approach, we can extrapolate behavior from a local context by highlighting social mechanisms across time through the longitudinal examination of spatial practices of our participants. The practices one engages in are simultaneously context specific and general behavioral patterns (Adler & Pouliot, 2011). Thus, practices represent repetitive social interactions with an environment through which conduct is understood and promulgated. The benefit of extending this to the digital sphere is that it introduces a new arena for social interaction unincumbered by traditional physical barriers of place, whereby new practices and social imaginaries may manifest. In short, examining practices shared across digital space and adopted by social entrepreneurs offers insight into the communications which protract or contract psychological distance and the role of space in this communication.

4.3 Insights from Our Netnographic Inquiry

Table 4.1 provides demographic and descriptive information regarding our participants' business orientation, age of venture, and country of operation, collected through semi-structured interviews and bi-weekly updates.

To capture the influence of the pandemic's stage on practices and account for the slow-onset nature of the COVID-19 crisis, our right-most column introduces the *(pre)lockdown* phase, which represents the existence of widespread COVID-19 concern and the beginnings of the lockdown period but not full lockdown. Only Hannah and Sally were interviewed before the COVID-19 lockdowns were conceived and they both pointed out the role of space in their ventures. Speaking about her biggest difficulties as a social entrepreneur, Hannah talks about her solitary work experience and space's role in overcoming it:

> My biggest challenge is I get lonely *laughs*. I know it sounds um like trivial, but I'm a massive extrovert... I can't afford a co-working space at this point, so that's not an option. Um, what I've started to do is on days where I don't have calls, I go and sit in a cafe and I have one or two friends who

Table 4.1 Overview of participants

Participant	*Country*	*Product v. Service*	*Age (of venture)*	*Stage at initial interview*
Hannah	UK	Service	0–1.5 years	Pre-Lockdown
Sally	UK	Product	1.5–3 years	Pre-Lockdown
Marshall	UK	Service	10+ years	Lockdown
Ruth	UK	Service	5–10 years	Lockdown
Lucy	UK	Service	3–5 years	Lockdown
Valerie	NL	Service	10+ years	(pre) Lockdown
Gerry	NL	Service	1.5–3 years	(pre) Lockdown
Laura	NL	Product	0–1.5 years	(pre) Lockdown
Winona	NL	Service	1.5–3 years	(pre) Lockdown
Joseph	NL	Product	1.5–3 years	(pre) Lockdown
Wilson	NL	Product	1.5–3 years	Lockdown
Beth	NL	Service	1.5–3 years	Lockdown
Max	NL	Product	0–1.5 years	Lockdown
Leanne	NL	Service	1.5–3 years	Lockdown
Cathy	NL	Service	1.5–3 years	Lockdown
Sandra	NL	Service	1.5–3 years	Lockdown
Jordan	NL	Service	1.5–3 years	Lockdown

> work remote or sometimes work from home, so we started to either, they come to my house and we work together, or we go into a café and we work together.

For Sally, place plays a big role in her ability to deliver her products to clients and maintain the consistency necessary to form a space for her venture, as she describes:

> …they provided us with a discounted rent for use of the kitchen and things like that…and they're happy to give you a room, but, you know, there was lots of issues with them taking bookings for the room we wanted to use on a regular basis, and you think 'well you can't run something if on the day that you turn up to have a lunch you suddenly, they've rented out your—*laughs* it needs to be consistent.

Indeed, COVID-19 notwithstanding, spatial availability emerged as areas of concern for Hannah, Sally, Valerie, Laura, Joseph, Beth, Leanne, Sandra, and Jordan during our interviews, and was brought up *within the context of COVID-19* by participants Marshall, Ruth, Lucy, Gerry, Wilson, Beth, Max, Cathy, Sandra, and Jordan. In our follow-up correspondence with Hannah and Sally, they too acknowledged the impact of lockdown and anxiety surrounding spatial constraints. In particular, RPs Sally, Laura, Joseph, Wilson, and Max reflected higher levels of uncertainty regarding the impact on space availability, presumably due to the product- oriented nature of their ventures. Through engagement with online space and bi-weekly updates, we currently identify 3 major themes of disruption caused by the COVID-19 lockdowns, which are addressed through spatial configurations: *Internal and reflexive engagement with venture; external engagement and product/service delivery; and venture repurposing and mission adoption.*

Internal and Reflexive Engagement. Despite our disagreement with the notion of the 'hero' entrepreneur, there are some characteristic traits attributed to a higher propensity for social entrepreneurship: particularly, trust and optimism (e.g. Praszkier et al., 2009). Indeed, optimism of a venture's potential in the face of uncertainty is a touted characteristic of the entrepreneur (c.f. Bandura, 1977; Drakopoulou & Anderson, 2007). When asked about a time where they felt too overwhelmed to continue, all of our participants enthusiastically admitted that they have had such experiences one way or another, and adopted different methods to ameliorate these internal feelings. Some turned to meditation while others turned to exercise, support groups, or 'unplugging' (see Calzada & Cobo, 2015).

As a once in a life-time crisis, the level of uncertainty imposed by COVID-19 served to disrupt participants internal loci of optimism. Cathy's social venture addresses labor force discrimination by training marginalized groups in the IT skills necessary for the twenty-first century economy. She described the feeling of hopelessness from no longer be able to hold in-person teaching sessions due to the lockdowns:

> ...we can switch to a digital model, we can do this and this and this, but these other things related to finance, are a huge problem because I have a payroll that I need to meet...because I really didn't see any way forward because it was like, I don't know how we're going to do this

As if in an instant, access to support groups, places for exercise, and even public spaces was revoked as a consequence of the lockdown restrictions. In addition, such spatial revocation initiated a reallocation of time and effort towards addressing personal commitments or addressing the social mission. In Cathy's case, she opted to increase the scope of her venture's social impact by engaging with the digital sphere, but was faced with significant challenges that emerged from operating in this digital space, which were coupled by the challenges presented by her students' at home personal commitments, as she describes:

> it was an all online model for the first three months, every day, I mean, Monday, Tuesday, Thursday, every day at 10 o'clock computers on, these are your peers, here's your teacher, your fellow coaches and your tutors—every day. The difficulty wasn't, it wasn't for lack of engagement opportunity, it was really, I mean, it was as much of being in the same space as we could. Um, but where it didn't work and where the breakdown is, is that it's really easy to hide online. So it's also really easy to get the right answers for the exam, but not know how to apply the knowledge. And when you are in a session where you need to apply the knowledge, it's extremely difficult online—and we are very focused on being able to apply that knowledge. In theory, learning online is fantastic, but if you can't actually do something with the learning then we've missed the boat because the goal is for you to be able to go to work. The goal is for you to make a difference at an employer. The goal is for you to grow and develop further while you're on the job, not to collect more diplomas. So what we saw was that being at home meant it's never just the individual that is learning, they're severely impacted by what's in their environment around them. Like one of our students came out and then later and said, I need some help because in my, at home I have three children and we live in, you know, we live in, in the middle of a community where people do not understand that I am studying, so I can't focus and I'm not able to apply these skills

Cathy moved to address these challenges by offering additional online group sessions to talk through the importance of setting boundaries despite the difficulties of no in-person interaction, which she explains derived from her own interpretation of overcoming the loss of in-person support:

> And I'm like, okay, well, here's where we're going to have to practice some boundary issues, setting some boundaries now, because this isn't going to get better. And it's, it's, it's impacting your future. And of course your family's future. And so, and then, so you see that there's all kinds of little things that are at play that make us hold people, but are not taken into account for what keeps the community strong. And when, and, and we saw this again and again and again, because it's also really easy to detach from your responsibilities to the community, if you're only digital... I like nothing better than

> also being at home, you know, where, and I mean, I take my dogs to my classroom to it. It doesn't matter, but, you know, it's like, yeah, I like using my own toilet and my own coffee machine and you know, all of the rest of this, but my community thrives by being together. So we need to work through this together.

For our participants with childcare commitments, we discovered during our bi-weekly correspondence that work for their ventures had ceased for weeks at a time due to child/family care. Sally, for instance, describes how the lockdown impacted her optimism for her venture's future, but she allocated her time to childcare commitments. As she writes in her diary, during August of 2020, the beginnings of the lockdown were not focused on her venture:

> But so far, looking after the girls full-time while schools are closed, I have spent no time at all working out how [venture] can re-open sustainably in this pandemic environment. The latest thinking, that catering for larger events was the way to go, is kind of obsolete. There are no weddings or large gatherings taking place for the foreseeable future. Corporates have most staff working from home so catering for office events and conferences is not a goer... so depressing!

In some cases, social entrepreneurs were left with no alternative but to change homes with significant implications for at-home work space. For example, in her diary, Laura describes how the impact to her business from COVID-19 forced her to move back home, with significant negative implications on how she was able to work at home, due to the problems of co-habitation:

> Due to the lockdowns, the government was like 'you can't anymore—you gotta stay inside' and no one wants to pay for anything anymore, either because the economy is so uncertain or whatever it is—especially freelancing and running your own business, like people are, people are just like firing people like crazy, no one's going to hire, or pay for contracts. Um, so that was actually the point at which I decided I had to move in with my parents... living with my parents affects how I work and my work definitely affects how I interact with my parents... even small things begin to irritate and stress me now, like the doorbell will be going off constantly and it makes it hard to concentrate.

In such instances, for Laura and for Cathy, the disruptions caused by COVID-19 negatively impacted time allotted to the entrepreneurs' ventures and perceptions of self-efficacy (Bandura, 1991).

External Engagement and Product/Service delivery. Incumbent upon social entrepreneurial activity is engagement with underserved demographics (e.g. Mair & Marti, 2009) and addressing the gaps which leave them behind (e.g. Mair et al., 2012). As with many crises, COVID-19 disproportionately impacts the underserved communities social entrepreneurs aim to help (HIMSS, 2022). Social entrepreneurs often adopt hybrid organizational formats in order to balance social value creation with economic viability (e.g. Austin et al., 2012; Nicholls, 2006); this dual identity serves to meet the need of all stakeholders of the organization by attracting multiple resources (e.g. Beckmann et al., 2014; Zeyen et al., 2014). Due to the spatial disruptions caused by COVID-19, it became difficult for our participants to manage their dual identities.

In addition to negatively impacting the internal loci which contribute to our participants' internal practices, disruption caused by COVID-19 extends outwards to impact the capacity of our participants to deliver their services or products and attract further resources. Indeed, the ability to go digital is a solution insomuch as the individuals in question have the capacity to go digital. Furthermore, our participants overwhelmingly indicated that in those instances prior to full lockdown they saw a paucity in physical engagement. As a consequence, Gerry, Joseph, Laura, Sally, Marshall, Ruth, Sandra, Leanne, and Max indicated a drop in revenue building activity while maintaining the same or seeing a slight increase in non-revenue activities. For example, Leanne runs a social venture based in Amsterdam which focuses on empowering marginalized groups with the skills to be part of systemic change. Due to the COVID-19 lockdowns they were unable to hold their in-person revenue-generating events. They opted to switch to digital, but operating in digital space did not exactly align with their social mission, as Leanne describes:

> ...with our event formats, we try to really make them relevant to people who are less privileged. Right before Corona, we were planning a public speaking event and it was about power dynamics and public speaking, and who gets to speak and why, and because of Corona we had to go virtual. But I'm not sure everyone will be able to get access, which is also connected to privilege.

To combat the inaccessibility of the online format, Leanne opted to hold a 9- week book club held on zoom which focused on issues of power dynamics. Through our netnographic involvement, we saw that the participants tended to be one of relative privilege—students from universities around the Netherlands and people who (self professedly) come from well-educated families. During a catch-up with Leanne, she describes her decision to discuss a book on power dynamics and marginalization:

> I grew up in a very political household and my parents pushed me to look at the underlying causes of things. That's the whole reason behind [venture], trying to get to the root of the problem. When I see how Corona has impacted everyone, but only a few people can make due, it really shows how widespread and misunderstood privilege is. Being in Amsterdam there are a lot of expats and university students that are really privileged who don't pay much attention to the underprivileged in Amsterdam. I think people have to understand their privilege so they'll be willing to help, there needs to be more discussion on what privilege looks like, so we decided to have this 9 week intense discussion sessions on how to recognize privilege and how the privileged can help those who do not have the same privilege.

Within this theme we see the biggest disruptions come because of the operational implications for the venture. That is, the loss of available space to our social entrepreneurs is felt in the way it inhibits the venture from fulfilling its revenue generating remit and pressures its economic viability, which, in turn, impacts their ability to subsidize their social activity.

Venture Repurposing and Mission adoption. Self-efficacy theory (Bandura, 1977, 1991, 1997) is notable for examining the behavior of entrepreneurial individuals, in particular, the behavior of serial entrepreneurs (see Hsu et al., 2017). While none of our participants are serial entrepreneurs (yet), this theme highlights shifts in participants behavior towards additional social value focused activities. 5 of our participants, through utilization of a shared digital space, participated in varying initiatives specifically emerging to support vulnerable groups during lockdown. Laura, Max, and Leanne engaged by tailoring their venture's activities to meet the needs set out by the initiating charities. Sandra and Jordan participated by utilizing their skills as volunteers of the charities participating in these COVID-specific initiatives. Laura and Winona participated in COVID-19 hackathons in addition to reorienting their ventures' activities to meet local challenges. For example, Winona participated in a COVID and grand challenges hackathon, which spurred her decision to support the local community through existing ventures. As mentioned in Chap. 2, Winona, for example, chose to support existing social enterprises to help the local community. She describes this shift in her diary:

> COVID definitely shifted things, so [hackathon] wouldn't have ever happened if there was no COVID. The purpose was on how to tackle challenges like COVID, but it wasn't just COVID. I actually worked on the use of energy and energy systems. I think the accumulation of all the things that I went through doing this and all they people I've met, that I might not have other wise met, really made me think that as a planet, as humans, we really need to shift the way we think, and we have a long way to go. And it's, it's the evolution of thinking. I think that is what we need to work on,...so I've been thinking on how best to help people and change their thinking.

Self-efficacy theory holds that success in previous entrepreneurial activities increases the propensity for subsequent entrepreneurial endeavors (Bandura, 2002). Furthermore, if previous ventures failed, or in the case of our participants, met significant external challenges outside of their control, we may expect them to maintain a higher propensity for involvement (Hsu et al., 2017). This theme is of particular interest as it highlights the power of our participants' social ethos, the social imaginary, and the generative capacity of space for actualizing behavior. That is, through the loss of physical space and subsequent difficulties identified in themes one and two, participants became involved in digital spaces where they engaged in additional socially directed behavior to replace their venture's temporarily suspended remit.

4.4 Space for Communicating Meaning

These findings suggest that the implication of spatial (re)configurations on social entrepreneurs extends beyond the boundaries of the economic sphere. Indeed, as the above themes show, the multi-faceted disruptions of COVID-19 impact the internal and external dynamics which give rise to our participants' practices. Here we discuss how the above themes relate to space, space-making processes, and the role of human and non-human elements.

Social entrepreneurial behavior extends beyond instrumental rationality and involves engaging with phenomena in ways that prove to be effective in the longer term, though the effectiveness may be unrecognizable in the short term (see Schumpeter, 1934). The articulatory capabilities of social entrepreneurs (see Beckmann, 2011) and their subsequent organizational capacity (Nicholls, 2006) enables them to initiate collaborative action necessary to alleviate social challenges (e.g. André et al., 2018; Powell et al., 2018) and particularly those which may emerge or be exacerbated during crisis (e.g. Chamlee-Wright & Storr, 2010, 2014; Dutta, 2017; Kraus et al., 2020). Social entrepreneurs act as sources of innovation (see Costales, 2022) for addressing the widespread loss of space due to crisis, as first movers whose behavior identifies where social challenges are emerging and how they could be addressed.

Spatial disruption engages the radical imaginary (see Castoriadis, 1977) of social entrepreneurs and alters their behavior to the extent that it enables socialization of this imaginary. Recalling the social imaginary, social and economic processes emerge from the shared beliefs, values, and norms in a given environment (Castoriadis, 1987). We hold that space is a medium through which the radical imaginary emerges, and place is the mechanism through which social and economic processes manifest and influence the social imaginary. Take Leanne, for example, who had a cognitive response to the spatial restrictions focusing on the meanings behind the underlying problems of society and how these problems might be addressed. To socialize these meanings in a way that aligned with her social mission, she created a place in the digital sphere where these meanings could be communicated, through the contraction of psychological distance. The dynamic nature of social and economic processes means that place is simultaneously the result of and a factor in spatial (re)construction. Indeed, social processes demarcate use and purpose of space (c.f. Goldhagen, 2017).

Sociomateriality holds that the social world emerges from a cyclical dance between humans and non-humans (e.g. Fenwick et al., 2015). In fact, they are mutually constitutive, and their dynamic relations set the foundations upon which practices are built (e.g. de Moura & Bispo, 2020). As it pertains to space, we must look to the bi-directional relationship between physical elements of place and social elements of space. Social entrepreneurs leverage this relationship in 3 ways: (i) to socialize their radical imaginaries and initiate a meaning-making process (ii) to manage norms to the extent they are not in opposition with the socializing imaginary and (iii) to manage the psychological distance of others.

In such instances where spatial constraints disrupt an entrepreneur's duty of care for themselves or others, it introduces a point of inflection whereby the internal mechanisms of balance and the radical imaginary may be disrupted. At this point an entrepreneur may seek out alternative spaces which enable them to reconcile their internal mechanisms with the cause of the spatial disruption. Where spatial constraints inhibit an entrepreneur's normal working practices or business operations, an additional point of inflection presents itself whereby they may seek out an alternative workplace. In pursuit of a new workplace, social entrepreneurs will seek out affordances which enable them to meet the remit of their venture or otherwise overcome obstacles in product/service delivery. In such instances where spatial disruption has a wide-scaled impact (such as COVID-19) and inhibits normal venture operations, in the absence of alternative spaces to regain operational normalcy, social entrepreneurs may opt to utilize their organizational capacity to address social ailments beyond the initial remit of their venture (such as in the case of Winona). It is at this point that we see the actualization of their changed imaginaries by looking to the social challenges they opt to address and the method by which they do so.

Figure 4.1 shows how the material and non-material elements of space influence the social entrepreneurial process. The impact of space on this process is not limited to the economic operations of social entrepreneurs' ventures. Indeed, it is felt at the individual level where social entrepreneurs take up their normative mission. Space therefore sits at the top of the figure as a metaphysical representation of the human capacity for individual autonomy, rational pursuit of goals, and endowing their environment with meaning. As such, space captures the internal dynamics which may instigate the value judgements that precede entrepreneurial action. It constitutes the medium through which they engage reflexively with their individual psychological distance and through which the radical imaginary emerges. Place is a mechanism through which the psychological distance of social entrepreneurs can manifest through their behavior. Place emerges from various economic processes external to the social entrepreneur, which involves mobilizing the factors of production (Mill, 1871); to the extent they utilize place, it is endowed with meaning and norms through the social and economic processes they undertake within this place. Indeed, place maintains constituent characteristics contingent upon the processes which led to its emergence; such material characteristics afford various social and economic processes. The social processes which emerge in this place may allow for the sharing of beliefs, norms, and promote collective behavior. Thus, additional space may emerge within bounded

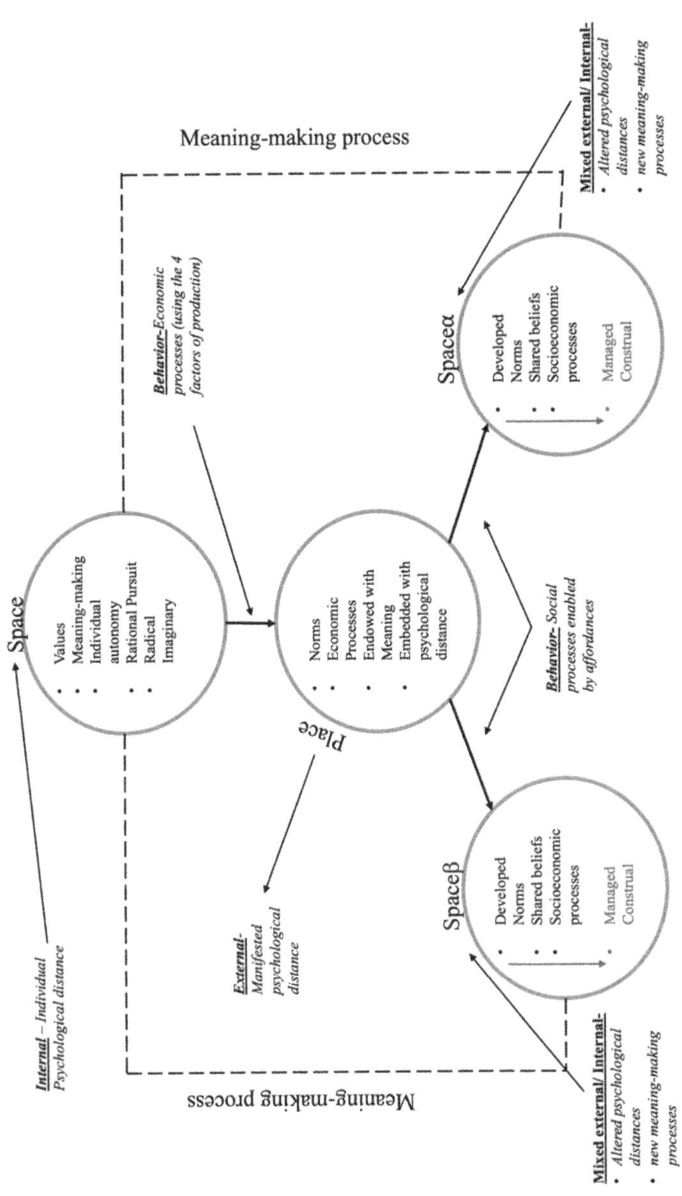

Fig. 4.1 The material and non-material elements of space in the social entrepreneurial process

place, where varying psychological distances can be managed, to the extent that they converge upon a shared imaginary. Indeed, Spaceβ and Spaceα serve to represent multiple additional spaces which may be present at any given time. Such additional spaces involved mixed levels of construal and internal reflection, and have the potential for elaborating human capacity. The elaboration of capacity links back to space to represent internal reflection with one's own psychological distance and initiation of new meaning-making processes.

As an example, let's take Starbucks as the place. Starbucks was constructed by mobilizing the factors of production to engage in economic processes such as sell coffee and baked goods. However, the materiality of the stereotypical Starbucks (such as tables, chairs, plugs) affords customers of Starbucks the opportunity to engage in varying social or economic processes (e.g. you can get a coffee and work or get a coffee and socialize). Contingent upon the processes undertaken, an additional space within the boundaries of Starbucks may emerge. That is, Starbucks may simultaneously be a workplace, a co-working space, a third-space, or a social space, contingent upon the meanings it has been endowed with. In the case of crisis, how a social entrepreneur reacts to the disruption of place (Starbucks) is a function of the social and material elements of the lost place (Starbucks). In fact, the prosocial nature of social entrepreneurship suggests that the meaning imbued by others may be similarly as impactful to a social entrepreneur's response to spatial disruption.

The data from our netnographic methodology suggests that social entrepreneurs engage innovatively with space as a tool of communication to protract or contract psychological distance and promote organizational behavior. It further suggests that, over time, the social interactions within these spaces form practices (structural coupling as Luhmann might refer to it) where the radical imaginary is socialized to the point it becomes a socially sanctioned symbolic network of functional and imaginary components (Castoriadis, 1987)—what Luhmann might refer to as interpenetration. Similarly, the data suggests that spatial disruption affects a social entrepreneur to the extent that it impacts their ability to manage psychological distances for the alleviation of social market failures. As they seek out affordances, there is equal possibility for carving out new spatial configurations.

Due to the inherent prosociality of social entrepreneurs, focusing on the responses of social entrepreneurs to spatial disruption, especially in times of COVID, was arguably the strongest method for capturing the extent to which space plays a role in communicating cognitive responses to the environment (people, economic systems, etc) as a means of addressing societal problems in the autopoietic society. Innovative use of space is by no means exclusive to social entrepreneurs, however. If we recall our discussion in Chap. 2, social entrepreneurs are complements to and supplements of the other innovative actors within society. That is, innovative communication from purveyors of social value requires the innovative communication of one another to achieve social change. The COVID-19 crisis has emphasized that there are significant elements of space—particularly its capacity as a medium of communication between people—that we have taken for granted, and which deserve to be better understood.

4.5 Where Do We Go from Here?

From a methodological perspective, researchers of all levels would benefit from incorporating a critical realist (ethno)netnographic methodology as laid out above, to construct a composite picture, detailing the nuances of multiple emerging spaces and the impact this has on rule-setting behavior. Particularly in the digital age, understanding the unseen elements of spatial configurations allows various disciplines to look to the future with a keener eye on how technology may impact work. Similarly, future research would benefit from examining responses to spatial constraints in contexts without strong digital infrastructure. Incorporating a critical realist (ethno) netnography will allow further research to shine light on motivations behind actions taken by purveyors of social value, beyond the social entrepreneur, and space's role in them.

The insights from our netnography primarily serve as an empirical case of how social entrepreneurs utilize space as a communicative tool for operationalizing the imaginary for societal change in the autopoietic society. Returning to grand challenges, how social entrepreneurs use space has larger implications for how wicked problems are understood and addressed due to the deep rooted and complex role that space plays in communicating meaning and value. Researchers of all levels who are interested in conducting research on wicked problems, grand challenges, or social innovation would benefit from implementing the spatial distinctions presented in this chapter and using it as a framework for analyzing the work practices of various purveyors of social value and how they engage with space. The ontological, epistemological, theoretical, and practical layering of this book so far has presented a research program which implements a novel view of space and can be easily adapted for aspiring or current researchers as widely as urban planning, economics, psychology, political science, social innovation, computer science, or sociology.

References

Acemoglu, D., Johnson, S., & Robinson, J. A. (2001). The colonial origins of comparative development: An empirical investigation. *American economic review, 91*(5), 1369–1401.

Adler, E., & Pouliot, V. (Eds.). (2011). *International practices* (Vol. 119). Cambridge University Press.

Agnew, J. (2011). Space and place. In *Handbook of geographical knowledge* (pp. 316–331). SAGE.

André, K., Cho, C. H., & Laine, M. (2018). Reference points for measuring social performance: Case study of a social business venture. *Journal of Business Venturing, 33*(5), 660–678.

Archer, M. S. (1995). *Realist social theory: The morphogenetic approach.* Cambridge University Press.

Archibald, M. M., Ambagtsheer, R. C., Casey, M. G., & Lawless, M. (2019). Using Zoom videoconferencing for qualitative data collection: Perceptions and experiences of researchers and participants. *International Journal of Qualitative Methods*, 18, https://doi.org/10.1177/1609406919874596.

Austin, J., Stevenson, H., & Wei-Skillern, J. (2012). Social and commercial entrepreneurship: Same, different, or both? *Revista de Administração, 47*(3), 370–384.

Ballon, P., Pierson, J., & Delaere, S. (2015). *Test and experimentation platforms for broadband innovation: Examining European practice.* Available at SSRN 1331557.

Bandura, A. (1977). Self-efficacy: Toward a unifying theory of behavioral change. *Psychological Review, 84*(2), 191.

Bandura, A. (1991). Social cognitive theory of self-regulation. *Organizational Behavior and Human Decision Processes, 50*(2), 248–287.

Bandura, A. (1997). *Self-efficacy: The exercise of control.* W.H. Freeman & Company.

Bandura, A. (2002). Growing primacy of human agency in adaptation and change in the electronic era. *European Psychologist, 7*(1), 2–16.

Banerjee, A. V., & Duflo, E. (2011). *Poor economics: A radical rethinking of the way to fight global poverty.* Public Affairs.

Bansal, P., & Knox-Hayes, J. (2013). The time and space of materiality in organizations and the natural environment. *Organization & Environment, 26*(1), 61–82.

Beckmann, M. (2011). The social case as a business case: Making sense of social entrepreneurship from an ordonomic perspective. In *Corporate citizenship and new governance* (pp. 91–115). Springer.

Beckmann, M., Zeyen, A., & Krzeminska, A. (2014). Mission, finance, and innovation: The similarities and differences between social entrepreneurship and social business. In *Social business: Theory, practice, and criticial perspectives*. Springer.

Bhabha, H. (1994). *The location of culture*. Routledge.

Bhaskar, R. (1998). Philosophy and scientific realism. In *Critical realism: Essential readings*. Routledge.

Blagoev, B., Costas, J., & Kärreman, D. (2019). 'We are all herd animals': Community and organizationality in coworking spaces. *Organization, 26*(6), 894-916.

Bouncken, R. B., & Reuschl, A. J. (2018). Coworking-spaces: How a phenomenon of the sharing economy builds a novel trend for the workplace and for entrepreneurship. *Review of Managerial Science, 12*(1), 317–334.

Branzei, O., Parker, S. C., Moroz, P. W., & Gamble, E. (2018). Going pro-social: Extending the individual-venture nexus to the collective level. *Journal of Business Venturing, 33*, 551–565.

Calzada, I., & Cobo, C. (2015). Unplugging: Deconstructing the smart city. *Journal of Urban Technology, 22*(1), 23–43.

Castoriadis, C. (1977). The French Left. *Telos, 1977*(34), 49–73.

Castoriadis, C. (1987). *The imaginary institution of society*. Mit Press.

Chamlee-Wright, E., & Storr, V. H. (2010). The role of social entrepreneurship in post-Katrina community recovery. *International Journal of Innovation and Regional Development, 2*(1–2), 149–164.

Chamlee-Wright, E., & Storr, V. H. (2014). Commercial relationships and spaces after disaster. *Society, 51*(6), 656–664.

Chen, H. S., Mitchell, R. K., Brigham, K. H., Howell, R., & Steinbauer, R. (2018). Perceived psychological distance, construal processes, and abstractness of entrepreneurial action. *Journal of Business Venturing, 33*(3), 296–314.

Costales, E. (2022). Identifying sources of innovation: Building a conceptual framework of the Smart City through a social innovation perspective. *Cities, 120*, 103459.

De Moura, E. O., & Bispo, M. D. S. (2020). Sociomateriality: Theories, methodology, and practice. *Canadian Journal of Administrative Sciences/Revue Canadienne des Sciences de l'Administration, 37*(3), 350–365.

Drakopoulou Dodd, S., & Anderson, A. R. (2007). Mumpsimus and the mything of the individualistic entrepreneur. *International Small Business Journal, 25*(4), 341–360.

Dutta, S. (2017). Creating in the crucibles of nature's fury: Associational diversity and local social entrepreneurship after natural disasters in California, 1991–2010. *Administrative Science Quarterly, 62*(3), 443–483.

Eyal, T., Liberman, N., & Trope, Y. (2008). Judging near and distant virtue and vice. *Journal of experimental social psychology, 44*(4), 1204–1209.

Fenwick, T., Doyle, S., Michael, M. K., & Scoles, J. (2015). Matters of learning and education: Sociomaterial approaches in ethnographic research. In *MultiPluriTrans in educational ethnography: Approaching the multimodality, plurality and translocality of educational realities*. Transcript Verlag/Columbia University Press.

Friedman, T. (2005). *The world is flat: A brief history of the twenty-first century*. Farrar, Straus and Giroux.

Garrett, L. E., Spreitzer, G. M., & Bacevice, P. A. (2017). Co-constructing a sense of community at work: The emergence of community in coworking spaces. *Organization Studies, 38*(6), 821–842.

Gibson, J. J. (1966). *The senses considered as perceptual systems*. Houghton Mifflin.

Gibson, J. J. (1986). *The ecological approach to visual perception*. Psychology Press.

Gieryn, T. F. (2000). A space for place in sociology. *Annual Review of Sociology, 26*(1), 463–496.

Goermar, L., Barwinski, R. W., Bouncken, R. B., & Laudien, S. M. (2020). Co-creation in coworking-spaces: Boundary conditions of diversity. *Knowledge Management Research & Practice, 19*, 1–12.

Goldenberg, J., & Levy, M. (2009). *Distance is not dead: Social interaction and geographical distance in the internet era*. arXiv preprint arXiv:0906.3202.

Goldhagen, S. W. (2017). *Welcome to your world: How the built environment shapes our lives*. New York: Harper.

Goldhagen, S. W., & Gallo, A. (2017). *Welcome to your world: How the built environment shapes our lives*. Harper.

Grant, A. M., & Berry, J. W. (2011). The necessity of others is the mother of invention: Intrinsic and prosocial motivations, perspective taking, and creativity. *Academy of management journal, 54*(1), 73–96.

Haeffele, S., & Craig, A. W. (2020). Commercial social spaces in the post-disaster context. *Journal of Entrepreneurship and Public Policy, 9*, 303–317.

Hampton, K. N., & Gupta, N. (2008). Community and social interaction in the wireless city: Wi-fi use in public and semi-public spaces. *New Media & Society, 10*(6), 831–850.

Healthcare Information and Management Systems Society (HIMSS) (2022). Industry Perspectives: Health Equity. [Online] Available at: https://www.himss.org/resources/industry-perspectives-health-equity

Hsu, D. K., Wiklund, J., & Cotton, R. D. (2017). Success, failure, and entrepreneurial reentry: An experimental assessment of the veracity of self-efficacy and prospect theory. *Entrepreneurship Theory and Practice, 41*(1), 19–47.

Jones, C., Lee, J. Y., & Lee, T. (2019). Institutionalizing place: Materiality and meaning in Boston's North End. In P. Haack, J. Sieweke, & L. Wessel (Eds.), *Microfoundations of Institutions. Research in the sociology of organizations* (Vol. 65B, pp. 211–239). Emerald Publishing.

Kingma, S. F. (2016). The constitution of 'third workspaces' in between the home and the corporate office. *New Technology, Work and Employment, 31*(2), 176–193.

Kozinets, R. V. (2002). The field behind the screen: Using netnography for marketing research in online communities. *Journal of Marketing Research, 39*(1), 61–72.

Kozinets, R. V. (2010). *Netnography: Doing ethnographic research online*. Sage Publications.

Kraus, S., Clauss, T., Breier, M., Gast, J., Zardini, A., & Tiberius, V. (2020). The economics of COVID-19: Initial empirical evidence on how family firms in five European countries cope with the corona crisis. *International Journal of Entrepreneurial Behavior & Research, 26*(5), 1067–1092.

Leca, B., & Naccache, P. (2006). A critical realist approach to institutional entrepreneurship. *Organization, 13*(5), 627–651.

Leonardi, P. M. (2012). Materiality, sociomateriality, and socio-technical systems: What do these terms mean? How are they different? Do we need them. In *Materiality and organizing: Social Interaction in a Technological World* (pp. 25–48). Oxford University Press.

Leonardi, P. M., & Barley, S. R. (2010). What's under construction here? Social action, materiality, and power in constructivist studies of technology and organizing. *The Academy of Management Annals, 4*(1), 1–51.

Liberman, N., & Trope, Y. (2008). The psychology of transcending the here and now. *Science, 322*(5905), 1201–1205.

Lô, A., & Diochon, P. F. (2019). Unsilencing power dynamics within third spaces. The case of Renault's Fab Lab. *Scandinavian Journal of Management, 35*(2), 101039.

Mair, J., & Marti, I. (2009). Entrepreneurship in and around institutional voids: A case study from Bangladesh. *Journal of Business Venturing, 24*(5), 419–435.

Mair, J., Marti, I., & Ventresca, M. J. (2012). Building inclusive markets in rural Bangladesh: How intermediaries work institutional voids. *Academy of Management Journal, 55*(4), 819–850.

Mill, J. S. (1871). *Principles of political economy: With some of their applications to social philosophy* (Vol. 1). Longmans, Green, Reader, and Dyer.

Moulaert, F., MacCallum, D., & Hillier, J. (2013). Social innovation: intuition, precept,concept. The International Handbook on Social Innovation: collective action, sociallearning and transdisciplinary research, 13.

Nicholls, A. (Ed.). (2006). *Social entrepreneurship: New models of sustainable social change*. OUP Oxford.

Norman, D. A. (1999). Affordance, conventions, and design. *Interactions, 6*(3), 38–43.

Office for National Statistics (ONS) (2020). Coronavirus and self-employment in the UK. Accessible at: https://www.ons.gov.uk/employmentandlabourmarket/peopleinwork/employmentandemployeetypes/articles/coronavirusandselfemploymentintheuk/latest

Ozimek, A. (2021). Freelance Forward Economist Report. Upwork. [online] Available at: https://www.upwork.com/research/freelance-forward-2021

Ohly, S., Sonnentag, S., Niessen, C., & Zapf, D. (2010). Diary studies in organizational research. *Journal of Personnel Psychology., 9*(2), 79–93.

Oldenburg, R. (1989). *The great good place: Cafes. Coffee shops, community centers, beauty parlors, general stores, bars, hangouts, and how they get you through the day*. Paragon House.

Orlikowski, W. J. (2007). Sociomaterial practices: Exploring technology at work. *Organization Studies, 28*(9), 1435–1448.

Orlikowski, W. J., & Scott, S. V. (2008). 10 Sociomateriality: Challenging the Separation of Technology, Work and Organization. *Academy of Management Annals, 2*(1), 433–474.

Patterson, K. D., & Pyle, G. F. (1991). The geography and mortality of the 1918 influenza pandemic. *Bulletin of the History of Medicine, 65*(1), 4–21.

Petriglieri, G., Ashford, S. J., & Wrzesniewski, A. (2019). Agony and ecstasy in the gig economy: Cultivating holding environments for precarious and personalized work identities. *Administrative Science Quarterly, 64*(1), 124–170.

Pouliot, V. (2015). Practice tracing. In *Process tracing: From metaphor to analytic tool* (pp. 237–259). Cambridge University Press.

Powell, E. E., Hamann, R., Bitzer, V., & Baker, T. (2018). Bringing the elephant into the room? Enacting conflict in collective prosocial organizing. *Journal of Business Venturing, 33*(5), 623–642.

Praszkier, R., Nowak, A., & Zablocka-Bursa, A. (2009). Social capital built by social entrepreneurs and the specific personality traits that facilitate the process. *Social Psychology [Psychologia Spoleczna], 4*(10–12), 42–54.

Schumpeter, J. A. (1934). The theory of economic development: An inquiry into profits, capital, credit, interest, and the business cycle. Cambridge, Mass., Harvard U. P.

Sen, A. (1999). *Development as freedom*. Oxford University Press.

Spinuzzi, C. (2012). Working alone together: Coworking as emergent collaborative activity. *Journal of Business and Technical Communication, 26*(4), 399–441.

Stephan, U., Uhlaner, L. M., & Stride, C. (2015). Institutions and social entrepreneurship: The role of institutional voids, institutional support, and institutional configurations. *Journal of International Business Studies, 46*(3), 308–331.

Storr, V. H. (2009). Why the market? Markets as social and moral spaces. *Journal of Markets & Morality, 12*(2), 277–296.

Täuscher, K., & Laudien, S. M. (2018). Understanding platform business models: A mixed methods study of marketplaces. *European Management Journal, 36*(3), 319–329.

Tremblay, D. G., & Scaillerez, A. (2020). Coworking spaces: New places for business initiatives? *Journal of Innovation Economics Management, 1*, 39–67.

Trope, Y., & Liberman, N. (2003). Temporal construal. *Psychological Review, 110*(3), 403.

Trope, Y., & Liberman, N. (2010). Construal-level theory of psychological distance. *Psychological Review, 117*(2), 440.

Wickham, R. E., & Knee, C. R. (2013). Examining temporal processes in diary studies. *Personality and Social Psychology Bulletin, 39*(9), 1184–1198.

Willis, P., & Trondman, M. (2000). Manifesto for ethnography. *Ethnography, 1*(1), 5–16.

Wright, A. L., Meyer, A. D., Reay, T., & Staggs, J. (2020). Maintaining places of social inclusion: Ebola and the emergency department. *Administrative Science Quarterly*. https://doi.org/10.1777/0001839220916401.

Yunus, M., Moingeon, B., & Lehmann-Ortega, L. (2010). Building social business models: Lessons from the Grameen experience. *Long Range Planning, 43*(2–3), 308–325.

Zeyen, A., & Beckmann, M. (2018). *Social entrepreneurship and Business ethics: Understanding the contribution and normative ambivalence of purpose-driven venturing*. Routledge.

Zeyen, A., Beckmann, M., & Akhavan, R. (2014). Social Entrepreneurship Business Models: Managing Innovation for Social and Economic Value Creation. In C.-P. Zimth & C. G. von Mueller (Eds.), *Managementperspektiven für die Zivilgesellschaft des 21. Jahrhunderts: Management als Liberal Art* (pp. 107–132). Springer.

CHAPTER 5

Deconstructing Social Entrepreneurship and its Role in Society

Abstract A Luhmannian view of systems helps us understand grand challenges differently. Seen through Luhmann's sociological perspective, we can argue that wicked problems arise due to the challenges of communication across social subsystems. Here, humans play a central role as they can enable structural coupling between subsystems, thereby alerting subsystems to such things as, for example, the need to cost for carbon emissions in pay/no pay codifications. Social entrepreneurship at its very core aims to disrupt the status quo by interrupting existing institutions or create institutions where voids existed. To dive deeper into this line of argument, this chapter makes use of ordonomics—an ethics approach rooted, in parts, in institutional theory which also incorporates Luhmannian thinking to deconstruct social entrepreneurship as a multi-layered process of disruption at society's micro, meso, and macro levels.

Keywords Social innovation • Social innovation model • Ordonomics • Social change • Social value • Institutions

Real change, enduring change, happens one step at a time
—Ruth Bader Ginsbrurg

E. Costales, A. Zeyen, *Social Entrepreneurship and Grand Challenges*, https://doi.org/10.1007/978-3-031-07450-9_5

5.1 Social Entrepreneurship as a Tool of Disruption

Returning to the concept of grand challenges and wicked problems, drawing insight from multiple parts of society is necessary for addressing societal problems by fully capturing society's innovative potential (c.f. Schumpeter, 1942). Furthermore, engagement with various sectors—specifically, combining and leveraging lived experience from previously disparate and marginalized groups—highlights how social entrepreneurship complements existing loci of (social) innovation (such as the market or state) by demonstrating the value of unifying social and economic objectives, and alerting the subsystems of society to such things as the need to cost for carbon emissions in pay/no pay codifications. Social entrepreneurship is fundamentally an activity which disrupts the communications of society and seeks to direct this disruption towards developing alternatives to current societal structures. When new societal structures form, we can say that (social) innovation has been achieved.

(Social) innovation tends to emerge as a learning curve from the repetition and contextualization of an idea to the point an idea becomes operational and manifests (c.f. Knight, 1967; Mulgan, 2007). Social entrepreneurs act as initiators of this learning curve by offering innovative solutions to social challenges by addressing perceived underlying problems rather than the symptoms (Dees, 1998; Costales, 2022). These issues are often addressed through the formation of social enterprises (e.g. Yunus et al., 2010). When the communications of the enterprise elicit a significant level of imitation, replication, and disruption, we can say that it has led to social change. Social change is therefore a codifier of a completed social innovation curve.

Since the rise of the modern welfare state in the 1960s and subsequent growth of social movements, the notion of social innovation has emerged in force. As a result, the term has widely become a catch-all for welfare provision, social inclusion, poverty reduction, and many other social issues (Moulaert et al., 2017). This catch-all use is due to the social innovation narrative calling for understanding, cooperation, and collective action (Moulaert & MacCallum, 2019). However, this catch-all implementation muddies the water between social value and social change, contributes to the obfuscation of social entrepreneurship's role within modern society, and overlooks the capacity of individuals for tackling wicked problems and grand challenges. Figure 5.1 illustrates this social innovation curve and the strata of society at which social value and social change emerge.

The differences between social value and social change are widely discussed in the literature (McMullen, 2011; Bagnoli & Megali, 2011; Bloom & Chatterji, 2009). In short, social value targets individuals and groups of individuals, while social change targets society at large (Hietschold et al., 2019). Social innovation has three fundamental elements which are vital to achieve social change: (i) addressing needs neglected by the market or state; (ii) creating new institutional relations; (iii) empowering people to transform existing structures (Moulaert et al., 2013). Thus, we can say that social value is a means of achieving social change by initiating the curve of social innovation, but social change (i.e. completion of this curve) is the end for social entrepreneurs (Dacin et al., 2010).

Social entrepreneurship, social enterprise, and social innovation tend to be conflated and subsequently misunderstood. While they have points of convergence, they diverge in that social entrepreneurship centers on the individuals, their characteristics, and motivation; social enterprise tends to focus on the mission of the organization that manifests from social entrepreneurial activity; and social innovation refers to institutional and social

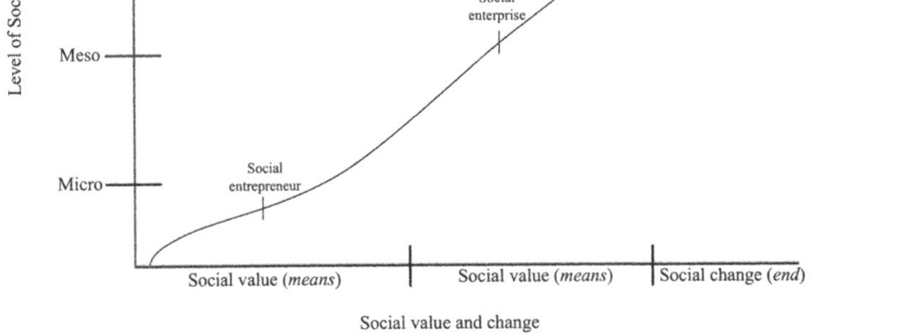

Fig. 5.1 Social innovation curve and corresponding societal strata

systems change that go beyond sectors to address social failures (see Westley & Antadze, 2010; Mulgan, 2007). The social innovation model of social entrepreneurship (Nicholls, 2010) allows us to make sense of this multi-level activity against the backdrop of the social innovation curve. This model of social entrepreneurship conceptualizes the process of social innovation as a means and an end for altering system configurations (Mulgan, 2012) and does not necessitate enterprise creation.

The social innovation model of social entrepreneurship captures and consolidates social entrepreneurship, social enterprise, and social innovation as three distinct phases in the social entrepreneurial process, operating at all three levels of society. It begins with the micro-level (social entrepreneurship), moves to the meso-level (social enterprise), and "ends" at the macro-level (social innovation). Within this model, however, social entrepreneurship does not 'succeed' based on the creation of a business—as is often the common interpretation. Rather, 'success' in this model is a function of the extent to which social innovation is implemented and adopted. It is therefore best to analyze this model as operating at the individual level, organizational level, and systems level of society. This stratified view illustrates how social change can be initiated at the individual level, diffused through the organizational level by various means, and how social innovation is incorporated at the systems level. In practice, social entrepreneurs create a social enterprise as a means of promoting and sustaining social value. To further develop this multi-tiered conceptualization of the social entrepreneurial process, we incorporate the ethics based theoretical framework of ordonomics.

5.1.1 A Brief Introduction to Ordonomics

While Luhmann can help us understand why society is complex as well as how changes in one subsystem may lead to adaptations in others, system theory often falls short in explaining how institutions that influence human behavior come about or which role they play. Ordonomics is a lesser-known approach to economic and business ethics (Pies et al., 2009). At its core, it aims to understand rule-setting and rule-taking within human interactions. To this end, it stratifies social interaction into three distinct levels. The basic game, the meta game and the meta meta game. Against this background, ordonomics offers a lens through which to examine the role of social entrepreneurship in society. The basic game refers to the daily interactions where people cooperate to meet their needs within a given set of rules (which we know as institutions). In the meta game, actors (individual or organizational) make decisions to optimize potential outcomes in the basic game through rule-setting behavior. For instance, social entrepreneurs who would not intend to change or disrupt the system but merely provide a social value, might aim to, for example, make education for marginalized children better within the given frame, and would be operating only at the level of the basic game. The meta game is the level at which actors reshape institutions and might engage in institutional work (e.g. Mair & Marti, 2009) or institutional entrepreneurship (Dorado, 2005) i.e. shaping new institutions or recombining institutions in previously unseen ways. The meta meta game refers to the level of semantic discourse where the benefits of cooperation are communicated to develop the shared understandings necessary for institutional change (Beckmann, 2011). This level is best thought of as the communication of ideas and perceptions of ideal conditions of cooperative behavior (Pies et al., 2010).

Achieving grand challenges requires reconciliation of the systematic disconnect between institutions and ideas, that characterizes the modern society (Pies, 2013). From an ordonomic perspective, the sustainable development goals (and other grand challenges) are semantic shifts in the way society conceptualizes the ideal relations between humans and their environments (social systems). Social entrepreneurship disrupts the current communications which lead to the disconnect between institutions and ideas by translating these disconnects at the individual and organizational levels to alert social systems to the need for new codifications, which ultimately lead to change at the systems level. During the process of translating these disconnects across societal strata, social entrepreneurs provide potential solutions to wicked problems that can be imitated and trialed across society.

5.2 The Individual Level as a Locus of Innovation

When we talk about the individual level of society, we are referring to independent persons or, as Luhmann might put it, the various combinations of autopoietic biological and psychic systems operating in the basic game. The social innovation model of social entrepreneurship presents these biological and psychic systems as the locus of multi-level social innovation. In the first instance, social entrepreneurs (like all actors in the basic game) are initially rule-takers—they interact within given institutions.

These institutions may be formal (such as codified laws) or informal (such as customs or other social norms) (North, 1991). Departing from the Schumpeterian notion that agents of innovation are not limited to any particular demographic of society (Schumpeter, 1939), the role of the social entrepreneur is one who communicates the deficiencies of these institutions for engaging optimally with the subsystems of society. All social entrepreneurs act in response to these perceived deficiencies in the structures of their environment. These perceptions are communicated through social interactions as a means of relaying the information of 'not enough' to disrupt existing interpenetrations by instigating rule-setting communications. Recall from Chap. 3 that interpenetration refers to the specific couplings of psychic and social systems to the extent that one (or both) systems treat one another like parts of their own system. In short, social entrepreneurs communicate to their environment (in this case people) that the current relations between them and the structures of their respective environments (social systems) are 'not enough'.

Since communication is only communication once information is perceived by the receiver (recall Fig. 3.2), social entrepreneurs implement innovative ways to impart this information of 'not enough' and the need for institutional rearrangement. This could be achieved through activity which demonstrates why something is 'not enough', or it could be done by contracting psychological distance through varying use of space. Let's take the example of the Grameen Bank (Yunus et al., 2010) to illustrate this individual level communication. Dr Muhammad Yunus began by micro-lending to the poor as an individual and discovered their untapped potential for entrepreneurial behavior when provided with opportunities presently unavailable to them by the banking structures of the economic system (see Yunus, 2017). Similarly, Leanne (Chap. 4) utilized a zoom space (due to the COVID lockdowns) to conduct various meeting groups to discuss lived experiences:

> What we tried to do is basically give people the tools to deconstruct what they're actually doing, because I think in lots of social impact spaces you have—yeah, the problem that there are people with great intentions, but who still operate within certain power structures, whether it be white supremacy, or god knows what. So what we try to do there is to kind of offer radical education formats, where people basically acquire tools to deconstruct their own position in society and what it actually means to make an impact. And that making an impact is often also a trade off.

In the former instance, Dr Yunus demonstrated the untapped potential of the poor to communicate the inefficient relations between them and the structures in the economic system. Specifically, the social norm of borrowing from the local moneylender and the formal lending requirement for collateral. In a similar vein, Leanne configured a digital space to bring people together and promote social interactions to communicate how various societal structures relate with marginalized people and demonstrate the inefficient relations between societal structures and marginalized demographics to illustrate the need for change. From the ordonomic perspective, the concept of social entrepreneurship is a semantic innovation due to these novel methods of articulation (such as those above) for communicating 'not enough' and initiating rule-setting behavior to disrupt current interpenetrations (see, Beckmann, 2011). By disrupting the relations between individual persons and the various structures of society, the individual level of the social innovation model is where lived experiences are operationalized to communicate systems shortcomings and question the relations between people and societal structures. In doing so, the social-innovation curve is initiated through an emphasis on reflexive agency which empowers people to communicate their place in society and mobilize to perturb the system and allow it to self-replicate with input from these novel perturbations.

5.3 The Organizational Level and the Social Enterprise

When we think of the organizational level of society, we tend to think simply of organizations and, typically, we think of companies such as Apple, Samsung, Walmart, Primark, JP Morgan, Facebook or Barclays. These are all organizations, but so too are governments, the local corner shop, the church, local community groups, universities, and hospitals. As it pertains to the social innovation model, 'organizational' refers to the organization of people with a particular purpose towards a unified end. This last part—a unified end—is very important for us. Building on the theory of autopoiesis, Morgan (2006) notes that social enterprises seek operational closure, perturbed by its environment, which initiates self-referentiation based not on a particular purpose, but a unified end. At first this distinction seems unnecessarily pedantic. What's the difference between a particular purpose and a unified end? How do we distinguish the two? And what are the implications of this distinction?

We distinguish a particular purpose and a unified end by the societal stratum at which they operate. A particular purpose is an individual-level unit of communication, while a unified end is, by its nature, an organizational-level unit of communication. For example, people work with various organizations to meet a variety of needs: maybe they need income, maybe they need some form of medical insurance, or perhaps they believe in the mission of the organization. In fact, these particular purposes are often studied as intentions (see Krueger et al., 2000; Koe Hwee Nga & Shamuganathan, 2010) or motivations (e.g. Baum & Locke, 2004; Germak & Robinson, 2014) for entrepreneurial behavior. By contrast, a unified end involves the unity of purpose directed at filling a gap left by the market or state, sometimes called organizational identity (Cornelissen et al., 2020; Nason et al., 2018). In short, a particular purpose refers to a solitary cognitive response to one's environment, while a unified end refers to the result of social interactions whereby multiple cognitive responses align to communicate mutually unaccepted environmental conditions.

If we return to Luhmann's definition of organizations as social systems which replicate on the basis of decisions (Chap. 3), we can then define social organizations as those that develop from a communication of 'not good enough' and self-replicate based on decisions regarding how to make something 'good enough'. As an example, social organizations such as charities, NGOs, social businesses, or social movements emerge to address a shortcoming in society's basic game which is communicated as 'not good enough'. We might expect that if the market or state provided adequate housing conditions then we would not need the UK charity Crisis.[1] If the market was immune to discrimination, we wouldn't need social enterprises such as Paz.ai[2] in the UK, or the Do Good Only Company[3] in the Netherlands. Similarly, if markets and the state were able to eliminate poverty, we might expect not to need the work of ActionAid,[4] an NGO operating across Africa, Latin America, and Asia.

The organizational level of society is therefore a social arena of the basic game whereby the players are organizations, which are "social" organizations to the extent that they live and die through communications of "not

[1] You can read about the Crisis charity here: https://www.crisis.org.uk/about-us/

[2] You can read about Paz.ai here: https://www.paz.ai

[3] You can read about the Do Good Only Company here: https://dogoodonly.nl

[4] You can read about ActionAid here: https://www.actionaid.org.uk/our-work

good enough". We can thus interpret this communication as disrupting the inefficiencies of the rules of the basic game. Social entrepreneurs engage in this organizational behavior to promote social value through the formation of their own organizations as the stewards of social value or organizing to influence existing organizations as stewards of social value (as is the case with social activism). Schultz (2009) points out that social organizations provide a "possibility space" where disruption is managed for prosocial ends, whereby people—beyond social entrepreneurs—can follow their desires to alleviate unacceptable environmental conditions. In fact, Archer (1995) distinguishes these organizational actors as those who are able to affect societal transformation precisely because of their organizational and articulatory capacity.[5] This articulation is the basis of rule-setting behavior (c.f. Beckmann, 2011).

Where does the social enterprise sit in this organizational arena? The social enterprise is perhaps best understood as a hybrid of the traditional nonprofit organization (Dart, 2004). In short, the social enterprise is a social organization created by the social entrepreneur, which combines business practices and a social ethos (Malki, 2009). Sometimes referred to as social ventures, double, or triple bottom line organizations (c.f. Dorado, 2006; Doherty et al., 2014; Santos et al., 2015), the concept has tended to manifest differently across contexts. For example, in the United States there is greater emphasis on earned-income strategies (Dees & Anderson, 2006; Defourny & Nyssens, 2010, 2012; Kerlin, 2006) and a favoring of the 'Social business' model as pioneered by Muhammad Yunus' Grameen Bank (Yunus, 2007, 2017; Yunus et al., 2010). In contrast, the European preference is towards a social sector emphasis (Defourny & Nyssens 2010, 2012; Kerlin, 2006). We can, perhaps, attribute this to the social contexts of the United States vs. Europe, particularly, the former's perception of the market's potential for addressing societal problems (c.f. Lepoutre et al., 2013). In either context, the twenty-first century society and globalization has blurred the lines separating the private, public, and non-profit spheres (Doherty et al., 2014; Durán-Romero et al., 2020; Leydesdorff, 2012; Mair et al., 2015).

The social enterprise stands out from the other forms of social organizations (such as charities or NGOs) in that it has emerged as the quintessential hybrid organization (see Battilana et al., 2017), which disrupts

[5] In her book *Realist social theory: the morphogenetic approach*, Archer refers to these actors as "corporate agents".

convention regarding economic and social organization as its unified end. In fact, much of the management literature surrounding the social enterprise is concerned with the maintenance of this unified end as it pursues various means for achieving it. The notion of mission drift is an inter-organizational disruption that emerges from undertaking various means (see Jones, 2007 for an overview of mission drift). As social enterprises seek to provide social value, they implement various market strategies as a means of remaining financially sustainable and, in doing so, often pursue conflicting institutional logics (Gümüsay et al., 2020; Smith & Besharov, 2019). Mission drift refers to the instances where the competing logics lead to organizational tensions, which cause the social enterprise to diverge from its unified end (Grimes et al., 2019). An unfortunate side effect of this mission drift is often founder departure, which has significant implications for the operationalization of the social mission (Bacq et al., 2019).

An additional distinguishing characteristic of the social enterprise is the social entrepreneur at the core of the venture. The social entrepreneur grounds the organization in their own pro-sociality and significantly influences the conduct of a social enterprise through the unity of purpose towards a unified end (Bacq et al., 2019). In this regard, the organizational level of the social innovation model refers to the social entrepreneur's organizational capacity and the social enterprise as an emergent tool for operating in the organizational arena to affect societal transformation and move along the social innovation curve. Thus, the organizational level is not concerned with the role of business, but rather how the dynamic process of social innovation disrupts the organizational status quo and perturbs the systems which govern society (Mulgan, 2007, 2012). In short, the organizational phase of the social innovation model is an additional means to meet social entrepreneurship's social innovation end by socializing individual level cognitive perturbations through the communication of "not enough".

5.4 The Systems level as an End

The social innovation model holds that social entrepreneurship is a multi-level disruptive process beginning at the individual level and 'ending' at the systems level. As such, it has social innovation as a means and an end. Social innovation as an end refers to social change: change in society's social systems whereby existing elements cross sectoral boundaries, new institutions are created, new relationships between disparate and marginalized groups emerge, and people are empowered to transform existing structures which opens the door for further innovations. As a means, social innovation refers to achieving at least two of the three fundamental elements presented by Moulaert et al. (2013); (i) addressing needs neglected by the market or state and (ii) creating new institutional relations. The social enterprise is a manifestation of (i); all social organizations emerge to address needs currently unaddressed or under addressed ("not good enough"). Similarly, as the social enterprise self-replicates through decisions for making a situation "good enough", it initiates new institutional relations through its hybridity, as directed by the social entrepreneur. This self-replication leads to perturbation of the subsystems of society within which they function (such as economic, judicial, or political) which, over time, leads to structural coupling between organizations and these subsystems to the extent that the information presented by the organization ("not good enough") is acted upon through the internal processes of a given subsystem.

Recalling the autopoietic system, the operative closure and interactional openness of the functional subsystems of society means that they can only change themselves, but they can be influenced by their environments. It is important to remember that this influence comes in the forms of perturbations which may initiate internal responses but cannot determine the outcome of this internal process—only the system's own structures can determine the outcome. The structures of the system emerge from the process of self-replication as a function of perturbations from its environment. These structures prime the system's replicative ability in response to future similar perturbations, and structural coupling emerges through iterative interactions and subsequent adaptability to the structures of the environment. The modern society, however, is anything but a vacuum: it is comprised of various systems, including people (see Fig. 3.1), all of which constitute one another's environments. Therefore, there are a variety of structures and structural couplings that form a resistance of sorts to the "not good enough" communication from the social entrepreneur and their enterprise. We call this resistance an immune response (Costales & Zeyen, 2022), which refers to a social system's (generally negative) reaction to disruptions in the basic game.

Our notion of the immune response is in keeping with the self-referential basis of the autopoietic society. If we think about the emergence of structural coupling and the operational functionality that follows, we can expect communications of "not good enough" to disturb the system's ability to self-replicate. For example, if structural coupling between the economic system and judicial system gives rise to charitable organizations (through 'charity' as a legal form and 'payment' of social service provisions from donations) we would expect that the emergence of the social enterprise, which makes a decision to adopt a legal form other than 'charity' and 'payment' of social service provision through donations and earned-income strategies, to face an immune response due to the friction against the structural coupling of the economic system (let's say the market) and the judicial system (let's say the legal form). In short, the market values a given product or service at a certain price while the legal form allows provision of the product or service at lower than market value (subsidized through donations)—how can these two be reconciled?

Social innovation as an end (social change) seeks to overcome these immune responses. The notion of functional differentiation of society's subsystems and the emphasis on functional institutions (Dimaggio & Powell, 1983; North, 1990) suggests that institutions emerge as rules for human engagement with the structures of these subsystems. The social innovation model emphasizes greater recognition of the symbolic components of institutions for overcoming systems' immune responses and affecting social change. The social imaginary introduces the fundamental notion that, while the systems of society may be functional in nature, the fundamental components of these social systems (humans) are not limited to functionality in the same sense. That is, systems change requires rule-setting behavior that consolidates the functional autopoiesis of society's systems and the symbolic nature of the psychic systems and cognitive responses of humans, with the notion that humans are environments to the system rather than part of the system. As such, social change represents disruption at the systems level to our current understanding of how systems operate and our role in their functionality. This view of the systems level as an end emphasizes the reflexive agency of the individual and highlights the underlying complexities of modern society which, if misunderstood, promulgate wicked problems. It further emphasizes the role of the communicating ideas (meta meta game) in social innovation.

5.5 The Ambivalent Toolbox of Social Entrepreneurship

When we speak of ambivalence in the context of social entrepreneurship, we mean that social entrepreneurship is good and bad as a function of the problems it aims to solve (see Zeyen & Beckmann, 2018). We return to the work of Adam Smith as a point of departure. In his 1759 book *The Theory of Moral Sentiments*, Smith introduced the concept of the invisible hand as a mechanism whereby positive economic and social outcomes may stem from self-interest fueled behavior (Smith, 2010). In *The Wealth of Nations* (1776), Smith built on these theoretical underpinnings and further analyzed the impact of self-interest fueled behavior, noting the negative outcomes of self-interest fueled behavior alongside the positive. The ambivalence perspective takes these two classical insights together and emphasizes the role of context in determining whether the outcomes are good or bad.

Returning to the individual level of the social innovation model, social entrepreneurs always act in response to a perceived deficiency in society's basic game. At this critical starting point, we have to ask ourselves how they come to perceive these deficiencies and how these perceptions initiate system changing communication. We may say that the complex interrelations between the social entrepreneur and their micro-cosmic and macro-cosmic environments elicits a cognitive normative response to their environmental conditions and what constitutes value (i.e. something *should* or *should not* be like this). We can also say that the value judgements within these responses emerge precisely because the various dual cosmos within which they belong forms their practical reality.

The ambivalence perspective primarily emphasis social entrepreneurship as a tool, whose effectiveness is a function of the problems attempting to be solved—which must first be identified (to an extent)—and how the tool is used to approach the problem. If we take the example of a hammer, we can say that the hammer is both good and bad and neither good nor bad depending on how it's used. Using the hammer to put a picture on a wall would generally be considered a good use, thereby making the hammer a good tool. Using the hammer to cut a hole in a shirt would widely be considered a poor use, thereby making the hammer a bad tool. In extreme cases, a hammer could be used to harm someone or it could be used to defend oneself. Who is to say whether it is good or bad? At its core, how something is used determines whether it is good or bad.

Recalling the propositions from Chap. 1, a fundamental challenge of wicked problems is that they have no definitive formulation, therefore we can only determine whether a tool is good or bad once the tool has been used (or in a trial situation). Take the wicked problem of poverty as an example. If social entrepreneurship is promoted as a tool for economic growth, the ambivalence perspective would question the relative efficacy of other tools (for example, traditional entrepreneurship or multi-national corporations are good facilitators of economic growth). If, on the other hand, social entrepreneurship is promoted as a tool for social value then the ambivalence perspective would view social entrepreneurship as a pretty good tool (though it would also question the viability of charities, NGOs, or social movements as alternatives). In this instance, the notion of poverty, what causes poverty, and what outcomes we want to see challenges our decision-making regarding the best tool to solve a problem.

The comparative nature of the ambivalence perspective grounds the multi-level disruption of the social entrepreneurship process against the backdrop of relative alternatives at each level of society to analyze its efficacy. These relative alternatives emerge due to the pluralistic society—who has value, what has value, and how best to achieve this is often a topic of fierce debate.[6] Is the best way to solve societal problems through existing organizations and institutional configurations or should we seek to develop new organizations and change institutional configurations? The ambivalence perspective seeks to clarify this question in an almost paradoxical way: both. Wicked problems are multi-faceted societal problems which are interpreted through a plurality of lenses and require existing organizational configurations and new organizational configurations. Let's take the example of a hurricane or other natural disaster. One may argue that philanthropy and governmental aid might be the best tools for providing immediate services and clean up. At the same time, however, social entrepreneurs, community activists, traditional entrepreneurs, and others provide value to the cause in a supplementary way (Chap. 2). In the aftermath and protracted post-disaster period, one may argue that philanthropy is less effective than, for example, social entrepreneurship (see Chamlee-Wright, 2007) due, in part, because the problem has shifted. While the goal is still to rebuild, social entrepreneurs may present stability in a way that philanthropy may not. This is not to say that philanthropy and governmental aid suddenly becomes useless, but it has now taken a back seat in terms of the 'best tool'. In short, the ambivalence perspective views

[6] See Zeyen and Beckmann (2018, pp. 50–53) for a detailed overview of such debates.

addressing societal problems like building a house. You can't build a house with only nails, you can't build a house with only hammers, and you can't build a house with only hammers and nails—it requires a variety of tools working in tandem, some more ideal at one point in time and less ideal at others.

With this in mind, thinking of social entrepreneurship as a toolbox presents social entrepreneurship as a complementary tool for society rather than a panacea for societal problems. As mentioned above, the social entrepreneurship process involves disrupting each level of society through a variety of communicative mechanisms. At the individual level, the social entrepreneur is the steward of disruption of the existing human-structure relations. At the organizational level, the social enterprise is the steward of disruption through the creation of disruptive space whereby traditional wisdom regarding economic and social organization is reconstructed, with the social entrepreneur as its north star. At the systems level, the systems themselves self-replicate on the basis of disrupted immune responses, initiated at the individual level and promulgated at the organizational level. Here, the disruptions of the individual and organizational level manifest as the systems of modern society adapt to the disruptions in their environments and form new structures. Over time, the process of structural coupling and interpenetration overcomes the deficiencies prior to the disruptions initiated at the individual level.

Combining the ambivalence perspective and the social innovation model of social entrepreneurship is a unique and novel lens for approaching the ideal end conditions of grand challenges due to its bottom-up, context specific, and iterative nature (c.f. Dacin et al., 2010; Lee, 2015). Disrupting societal relations at each level has the benefit of identifying ideal tools against the backdrop of contextual conditions and the iterative nature of the social entrepreneurship process primes various systems configurations for perturbations that are not limited to the social entrepreneur. In short, the ambivalent toolbox of social entrepreneurship contains a variety of tools for creating disruption (such as the social enterprise at the organizational level and questioning the relations between people and societal structures at the individual level) and primes societal structures for future perturbations from existing organizations and institutional configurations as they create disruption. In this way, social entrepreneurship not only tests the water for potentially ideal tools to address wicked problems, but it sets the stage for social systems configurations, which would be necessary to achieve the end conditions of grand challenges.

References

Archer, M. S. (1995). Realist social theory: The morphogenetic approach. Cambridge university press.

Bacq, S., Janssen, F., & Noël, C. (2019). What happens next? A qualitative study of founder succession in social enterprises. *Journal of Small Business Management, 57*(3), 820–844.

Bagnoli, L., & Megali, C. (2011). Measuring performance in social enterprises. *Nonprofit and Voluntary Sector Quarterly, 40*(1), 149–165.

Battilana, J., Besharov, M., & Mitzinneck, B. (2017). On hybrids and hybrid organizing: A review and roadmap for future research. In R. Greenwood, C. Oliver, T. E. Lawrence, & R. E. Meyer (Eds.), *The SAGE handbook of organizational institutionalism* (pp. 128–162). Sage.

Baum, J. R., & Locke, E. A. (2004). The relationship of entrepreneurial traits, skill, and motivation to subsequent venture growth. *Journal of Applied Psychology, 89*(4), 587.

Beckmann, M. (2011). The social case as a business case: Making sense of social entrepreneurship from an ordonomic perspective. In Corporate citizenship and new governance (pp. 91–115). Dordrecht: Springer.

Bloom, P. N., & Chatterji, A. K. (2009). Scaling social entrepreneurial impact. *California Management Review, 51*(3), 114–133.

Chamlee-Wright, E. (2007). The long road back: Signal noise in the post-Katrina context. *The Independent Review, 12*(2), 235–259.

Cornelissen, J. P., Akemu, O., Jonkman, J. G., & Werner, M. D. (2020). Building character: The formation of a hybrid organizational identity in a social enterprise. *Journal of Management Studies, 58*, 1294–1330.

Costales, E. (2022). Identifying sources of innovation: Building a conceptual framework of the Smart City through a social innovation perspective. *Cities, 120*, 103459.

Costales, E., & Zeyen, A. (2022). *Social Capital and the Morphogenesis of Actors: Lessons from International Social Entrepreneurs.* In The International Dimension of Entrepreneurial Decision-Making (pp. 193–222). Springer, Cham.

Dacin, P. A., Tina Dacin, M., & Matear, M. (2010). Social entrepreneur- ship: Why We don't need a new theory and how we move forward from here. *Academy of Management Perspectives, 24*, 37–58.

Dart, R. (2004). The legitimacy of social enterprise. *Nonprofit Management and Leadership, 14*(4), 411–424.

Dees, J. G. (1998). The meaning of social entrepreneurship. Fuqua School of Business Dukes University, 1–6.

Dees, J. G., & Anderson, B. B. (2006). Framing a theory of social entrepreneurship: Building on two schools of practice and thought. *Research on social entrepreneurship: Understanding and contributing to an emerging field, 1*(3), 39–66.

Defourny, J., & Nyssens, M. (2010). Conceptions of social enterprise and social entrepreneurship in Europe and the United States: Convergences and divergences. *Journal of Social Entrepreneurship, 1*, 32–53.

Defourny, J., & Nyssens, M. (2012). Conceptions of social enterprise in Europe: A comparative perspective with the United States. In *Social enterprises* (pp. 71–90). Palgrave Macmillan.

DiMaggio, P. J., & Powell, W. W. (1983). The Iron Cage Revisited: Institutional Isomorphism and Collective Rationality in Organizational Fields. *American Sociological Review, 48*(2), 147–160. https://doi.org/10.2307/2095101

Doherty, B., Haugh, H., & Lyon, F. (2014). Social enterprises as hybrid organizations: A review and research agenda. *International Journal of Management Reviews, 16*(4), 417–436.

Dorado, S. (2005). Institutional entrepreneurship, partaking, and convening. *Organization Studies, 26*(3), 385–414.

Dorado, S. (2006). Social entrepreneurial ventures: Different values so different process of creation, no? *Journal of Developmental Entrepreneurship, 11*(04), 319–343.

Durán-Romero, G., López, A. M., Beliaeva, T., Ferasso, M., Garonne, C., & Jones, P. (2020). Bridging the gap between circular economy and climate change mitigation policies through eco-innovations and Quintuple Helix Model. *Technological Forecasting and Social Change, 160*, 120246.

Germak, A. J., & Robinson, J. A. (2014). Exploring the motivation of nascent social entrepreneurs. *Journal of Social Entrepreneurship, 5*(1), 5–21.

Grimes, M. G., Williams, T. A., & Zhao, E. Y. (2019). Anchors aweigh: The sources, variety, and challenges of mission drift. *Academy of Management Review, 44*, 819–845.

Gümüsay, A. A., Smets, M., & Morris, T. (2020). "God at work": Engaging central and incompatible institutional logics through elastic hybridity. *Academy of Management Journal, 63*, 124–154.

Hietschold, N., Voegtlin, C., Scherer, A. G., & Gehman, J. (2019). What we know and don't know about social innovation: A multi-level review and research agenda. In *Academy of Management Proceedings* (p. 12332). Academy of Management.

Jones, M. B. (2007). The multiple sources of mission drift. *Nonprofit and Voluntary Sector Quarterly, 36*(2), 299–307.

Kerlin, J. A. (2006). Social enterprise in the United States and Europe: Understanding and learning from the differences. *Voluntas: International Journal of Voluntary and Nonprofit Organizations, 17*(3), 246–262.

Koe Hwee Nga, J., & Shamuganathan, G. (2010). The influence of personality traits and demographic factors on social entrepreneurship start up intentions. *Journal of Business Ethics, 95*(2), 259–282.

Knight, K. E. (1967). A descriptive model of the intra-firm innovation process. *The journal of business, 40*(4), 478–496.

Krueger, N. F., Jr., Reilly, M. D., & Carsrud, A. L. (2000). Competing models of entrepreneurial intentions. *Journal of Business Venturing, 15*(5–6), 411–432.

Lee, I. (2015). A social enterprise business model for social entrepreneurs: Theoret-ical foundations and model development. *International Journal of Social Entre- preneurship and Innovation, 3*(4) www.inderscienceonline.com/doi/abs/10.1504/IJSEI.2015.069351

Lepoutre, J., Justo, R., Terjesen, S., & Bosma, N. (2013). Designing a global standardised methodology for meas- uring social entrepreneurship activity: The Global Entrepreneurship Monitor social entrepreneurship study. *Small Business Economics, 40*, 693–714.

Leydesdorff, L. (2012). The triple helix, quadruple helix,..., and an N-tuple of helices: Explanatory models for analyzing the knowledge-based economy? *Journal of the Knowledge Economy, 3*(1), 25–35.

Mair, J., & Marti, I. (2009). Entrepreneurship in and around institutional voids: A case study from Bangladesh. *Journal of Business Venturing, 24*(5), 419–435.

Mair, J., Mayer, J., & Lutz, E. (2015). Navigating institutional plurality: Organizational governance in hybrid organizations. *Organization Studies, 36*(6), 713–739.

Malki, S. (2009). Social entrepreneurship and complexity models. In J. A. Goldstein, J. K. Hazy, & J. Silberstang (Eds.), *Complexity Science and Social Entrepreneurship: Adding social value through systems thinking* (pp. 71–81). ISCE Pub.

McMullen, J. S. (2011). Delineating the domain of development entrepreneurship: A market–based approach to facilitating inclusive economic growth. *Entrepreneurship Theory and Practice, 35*(1), 185–215.

Morgan, G. (2006). Images of Organization,(updated edn). Thousand Oaks, CA and London: Sage.

Moulaert, F., MacCallum, D., & Hillier, J. (2013). Social innovation: Intuition, precept, concept. In *The international handbook on social innovation: Collective action, social learning and transdisciplinary research* (pp. 13–24). Edward Elgar Publishing.

Moulaert, F., Mehmood, A., MacCallum, D., & Leubolt, B. (2017). Social innovation as a trigger for transformations-the role of research. Publications Office of the European Union.

Moulaert, F., & MacCallum, D. (2019). *Advanced introduction to social innovation*. Edward Elgar Publishing.

Mulgan, G. (2007). Social innovation what it is, why it matters and how it can be accelerated (Vol. 22). *Skoll Centre for social entrepreneurship*. https://doi.org/10.1515/zna-1967-1247

Mulgan, G. (2012). The theoretical foundations of social innovation. In *Social innovation* (pp. 33–65). Palgrave Macmillan.
Nason, R. S., Bacq, S., & Gras, D. (2018). A behavioral theory of social performance: Social identity and stakeholder expectations. *Academy of Management Review, 43*, 259–283.
Nicholls, A. (2010). The legitimacy of social entrepreneurship: Reflexive isomorphism in a pre-paradigmatic field. *Entrepreneurship Theory and Practice, 34*(4), 611–633.
North, D. C. (1990). *Institutions, institutional change and economic performance.* Cambridge University Press.
North, D. C. (1991). Institutions. *Journal of economic perspectives, 5*(1), 97–112.
Pies, I. (2013). The ordonomic approach to order ethics (No. 2013–20). Martin Luther University of Halle-Wittenberg, Chair of Economic Ethics.
Pies, I., Hielscher, S., & Beckmann, M. (2009). Moral commitments and the societal role of business: An ordonomic approach to corporate citizenship. *Business Ethics Quarterly, 19*(3), 375–401.
Pies, I., Beckmann, M., & Hielscher, S. (2010). Value creation, management competencies, and global corporate citizenship: An ordonomic approach to business ethics in the age of globalization. *Journal of Business Ethics, 94*(2), 265–278.
Santos, F., Pache, A. C., & Birkholz, C. (2015). Making hybrids work: Aligning business models and organizational design for social enterprises. *California Management Review, 57*(3), 36–58.
Schultz, R. (2009). In J. A. Goldstein, J. K. Hazy, & J. Silberstang (Eds.), *"Preface-social business: Designing the possibility space for social action". Complexity science and social entrepreneurship: Adding social value through systems thinking* (pp. 1–8). ISCE Pub.
Schumpeter, J. A. (1939). *Business cycles* (Vol. 1, pp. 161–174). McGraw-Hill.
Schumpeter, J. A. (1942). *Capitalism, socialism and democracy.* Routledge.
Smith, A. (1776). *An inquiry into the nature and the causes of the wealth of nations. The Glasgow edition of the works and correspondence of Adam Smith.* Reprint 20. Palgrave Macmillan. https://doi.org/10.1057/9780230291652.
Smith, A. (2010). *The theory of moral sentiments.* Penguin.
Smith, W. K., & Besharov, M. L. (2019). Bowing before dual gods: How structured flexibility sustains organizational hybridity. *Administrative Science Quarterly, 64*, 1–44.
Westley, F., & Antadze, N. (2010). Making a difference: Strategies for scaling social innovation for greater impact. *Innovation Journal, 15*(2).
Yunus, M. (2007). Creating a world without poverty: Social business and the future of capitalism. Public affairs.
Yunus, M. (2017). A world of three zeros: The new economics of zero poverty, zero unemployment, and zero net carbon emissions.

Yunus, M., Moingeon, B., & Lehmann-Ortega, L. (2010). Building social business models: lessons from the Grameen experience. *Long Range Planning, 43*(2–3), 308–325.
Zeyen, A., & Beckmann, M. (2018). Social Entrepreneurship and Business Ethics: Understanding the Contribution and Normative Ambivalence of Purpose-driven Venturing. Routledge.

CHAPTER 6

The Sustainable Development Goals, Complexity, and Errors of the Third Kind

Abstract As we pursue grand challenges, solutions to wicked problems continue to be elusive. As described in Chap. 1, wicked problems cannot be solved through traditional processes because they are unclear and complex in nature. As we seek to find solutions, how we define and conceptualize societal problems contributes to our ability to solve them and meet grand challenges. This chapter introduces the concept of type III errors as a lens for further analyzing the role of social entrepreneurship for meeting grand challenges. We take a deep dive into some of the wicked problems obfuscating our achievement of SDGs 1, 8 and 13, and how they practically relate to grand challenges. In doing so, we re-conceptualize them through the lens of multi-layered disruption and ambivalence to identify inflection points where errors of the third kind emerge, how they might be avoided or learned from, and social entrepreneurship's role in this process. In short, we end our journey with an academic plea for changing the world through individual- level changes.

Keywords Type III errors • Wicked problems • Grand challenges • Sustainable development goals

E. Costales, A. Zeyen, *Social Entrepreneurship and Grand Challenges*, https://doi.org/10.1007/978-3-031-07450-9_6

We but mirror the world. All the tendencies present in the outer world are to be found in the world of our body. If we could change ourselves, the tendencies in the world would also change
—Mahatma Gandhi

6.1 Errors of the Third Kind

When we speak about errors of the third kind (type III errors), we are referring to "the error committed by giving the right answer to the wrong problem" (Kimball, 1957, p. 134). For example, let's take Kenya's 2011 'Laptops for School' initiatives.[1] The idea was to reorient Kenya's educational system to be more digitally intensive and prepare students for an ICT (information communication technology) intensive economy by providing them with laptops and tablets. Promoting digital literacy is undoubtedly a good idea for thriving in the twenty-first century knowledge economy, but the initiative ultimately failed, in part because the educators themselves didn't have the necessary digital literacy. In short, the solution was correct—ICT and computers/tablets are phenomenal supplements for in-school education to prepare students for the twenty-first century economy, against the backdrop of a strong foundation of trained educations, a functioning school system, and available internet access. In this instance, however, the solution was to the wrong problem. The 'right' problem(s) (to focus on) was the relatively low school attendance or trained educators. Put another way, errors of the third kind are due to misrepresentations of a given problem—we think the problem is X, but the problem is actually Y. Therefore, any solution we come up with for X (no matter how good our solutions are) won't solve our problem. If we pay attention, however, type III errors have a way of shedding light on why the error occurred and offer a potential pathway towards a successful appropriate solution. In her book *The Charisma Machine* (2019), Morgan Ames identified the pitfalls of the One Laptop per Child model—an approach adopted by Kenya's Laptops for School initiative—by highlighting the misrepresentations of the problem being addressed, in this case, an emphasis on "the imaginary of the technically precocious boys… enthusiastically engaging with [the] programs" (p. 120) that simply did not align

[1] The Guardian provides an overview of the initiative here: https://www.theguardian.com/global-development/poverty-matters/2013/jun/27/kenya-laptops-schools

with practical uses on the ground. There are valuable lessons to be taken away from the failure of Kenya's Laptops initiative, the dissolution of the One Laptop Per Child foundation, and the insights from Ames' work, particularly, to be cautious of utopian promises of technological implementation. But more importantly, projects such as this first require a strengthening of the foundations upon which technology can stand. An example of these learnings is ACS International's 'laptop drop' initiative to enhance distance learning across 20 primary schools during the COVID-19 pandemic.[2] While it's important to note that this initiative was conducted in the United Kingdom, operationally, they approached the initiative from multiple directions, one of which was to provide teacher training and avoid the errors of technological determinism in education (see Oliver, 2011 for an overview of the relationship between technology and education).

The type III error has its origins in mathematics, particularly the statistical paradigm of accepting vs rejecting a null hypothesis. To take a step back, an error of the first kind results from rejecting a null hypothesis when it is true (a false positive), while an error of the second kind results from accepting a null hypothesis when it is false (a false negative). Mathematically, an error of the third kind results from correctly rejecting the null hypothesis for the wrong reasons, generally an incorrect inference regarding the directionality of the result (Onwuegbuzie & Daniel, 2003). Extrapolating this beyond a mathematical context, and into the wicked problem discussion, we can see how an incorrect inference of a result stems from a misinterpretation of the problem in question (c.f. Adler et al., 2016). In developing his definition, Kimball drew on errors emerging in practical consulting contexts and determined that the type III error is fundamentally a communication problem between the parties working together to address a problem (Kimball, 1957).

Such problems of communication tend to emerge from asking the wrong questions. That is, questions that have little to do with the underlying problem. If we take the wicked problem of poverty, as an example, a reasonable first step might be to ask: is there a relationship between poverty and crime? We can say with a good deal of certainty that the answer is "yes, there is". Let's say we then ask ourselves: "do we see less crime in

[2] The partnership director at ACS International has posted a blog about the initiative here: https://www.isc.co.uk/media-enquiries/isc-blogs/spotlight-on-acs-international-schools-laptops-for-learning-initiative/

countries (or areas) with lower levels of poverty?" Again, we might reasonably assume that the answer is "yes, we do". Where do we go from here? To move on from this stage, in terms of practically addressing the problem, we must first take a stance regarding the directionality of these correlations as a point of departure for the allocation of time or resources, bearing in mind that people of all socio-economic backgrounds commit crimes and vice versa. Simply being poor does not make one prone to crime the same way being wealthy does not inhibit criminal activity. We can then fairly assume that crime and poverty may be causal factors to one another but are by no means *the* cause of one another.

In this instance, the type III error occurs when a directional causality is attributed as *the* cause and leads to one of the following 'solutions': addressing (only) poverty to alleviate crime, or addressing (only) crime to alleviate poverty. It's important to note that, in this case, the type III error is not the emerging 'solution' but rather the confines of the solution set forth by the (mis)representation of a single (or wrong) causality, which leads to a cascade of additional errors of the third kind.[3] Addressing crime as a means of alleviating poverty and addressing poverty as a means of alleviating crime are perfectly reasonable and rational solutions for moving towards the grand challenge of 'no poverty' (SDG 1). However, type III errors cause a myopic view of a situation and overemphasis on improper solutions which lead to further errors of the third kind. For example, in an extreme case, representing poverty as *the* cause of crime would suggest that giving everyone a certain amount of money would put a halt to crime, and representing crime as *the* cause of poverty suggests that incarcerating all criminals would raise people out of poverty. This would then lead to resource allocation directed at either giving everyone money or putting all criminals in jail, which would amount to an insufficient and ultimately wasteful use of funds. After all, how would giving everyone money stop criminal activity or imprisoning all criminals lift all people out of poverty? Such actions (tighter control on crime and enhanced economic opportunity) must be supplemented by increased spending on education, for example.

[3] We use this wording of 'single (or wrong)' because the definition of the type III error is specifically regarding solving the wrong problem, but the wicked nature of the problem of poverty means that we cannot say definitively that the causality in the given example is 'wrong', but rather that the cause of poverty is not limited to crime and vice versa.

In a more realistic example, let's return to Kenya's Laptops for School initiative. In this instance, the desired outcome was to output the next generation of workers for the digital economy and overcome an existing shortcoming in the quality of digital learning. The problem of this shortcoming was conceptualized as one of a lack of access to computers and tablets in the classroom. As such, a significant amount of money was allocated to this purpose: trying to transition to a digitally focused educational system and away from the training of teachers, equitable access to education, and even clean water provision. In this case, the initial type III error emerged from the misrepresentation of the underlying problem as the (lack of) availability of computers and tablets. Subsequent errors of the third kind emerged from the misrepresentation of technology as a substitute to instead of a supplement of education and the allocation of over £200m towards laptop provision without the necessary teaching force. Understanding how errors of the third kind emerge is foundational to systemic thinking and problem solving by considering the impact of value judgements on the (mis)representation of a given problem and subsequent solutions emerging from this initial (mis)representation (Mitroff & Featheringham, 1974). Recall from Chap. 5, social entrepreneurship is initiated on the basis of value judgements in society's basic game. Thus, fundamental to understanding social entrepreneurship's role in meeting grand challenges is how they learn from and avoid type III errors.

A vital starting point for avoiding type III errors is the reality of pluralism in the modern society. In short, pluralism refers to the notion that people hold multiple perspectives as a function of the dual cosmos and, in particular, the variety of 'groups' to which they belong. It also means that members of the same 'group' are by no means required to have aligning views. As touched upon above, a type III error arises once a decision is made regarding what is important to achieve, of the available options. In the Laptops for School example, the decision was made that having laptops was more important than trained teachers for outputting the next generation of workers for the knowledge economy. The fact of pluralism begs the question: more important to whom? If we further examine the Laptops for Schools decision, we might reasonably argue that all parties involved might not deem the provision of laptops as the more important decision. For example, the students might have chosen access to clean water, teachers may have chosen to address widespread poor attendance, and government officials may have chosen providing laptops due to the optics. This variety of perspective and opinion gives rise to (mis) representations of a given problem. When we think about grand challenges, specifically the sustainable development goals, it is fair to say that these are ambitious—near utopian—ideal end conditions that most people can agree on. The value judgements behind each of the 17 SDGs are mostly uncontroversial: no poverty, zero hunger, reduced inequalities, and responsible consumption are fairly easy to understand; in a pluralistic world, however, the 'why' is different across parties involved. For those directly impacted by poverty, inequality, hunger, and (ir)responsible consumption, we might surmise that the 'why' is linked to an increased quality of life. For those indirectly impacted, we might surmise that the 'why' is linked to a variety of moral obligations or self-interest. This impact of pluralism is furthered by the 'how'. Against the backdrop of modern society, how do we begin moving towards these end conditions?

As we pursue these ideal end conditions, type III errors tend to emerge from ignorance at the micro, meso, and macro levels of society. The complexities of the modern pluralistic society necessitate a balancing act between the cosmos for different end conditions. For example, group A and group B might both agree on SDG 1 (no poverty), but fundamentally disagree on how to achieve this. At the same time, members of group A and group B may perfectly align on methods of achieving this end condition because they may be part of group AB. To further complicate the matter, a member of group AB might disagree with another member of group AB because solidarity to group A or B may compel them to move away from group AB. An error of the third kind emerges from the decision to effectively prioritize group A, B, or AB's individual microcosmic logics and attempt large scale solutions which involve the cooperation of group A, B, and AB dynamics. In this instance of the SDGs, the initial type III error is the representation of ideal societal end conditions as de facto acceptance across society's various dual cosmos. This leads to subsequent type III errors in the means for achieving these conditions within the same boundaries the ideal conditions were conceived. As such, systemic barriers to grand challenges and wicked problems emerge due to misrepresentation of the underlying problems. As an example, SDG 8 (decent work and economic growth) is broken down into twelve subgoals based on traditional conceptualizations of economic growth, such as gross domestic product (GDP). Even the notion of emphasizing economic growth as a prerequisite for ideal societal conditions can be reasonably argued against (see Piketty, 2014; Raworth, 2017). While there are vague mentions of innovation, entrepreneurship, and involvement of civil society, there is no mention of social entrepreneurship in the UN resolution (UNGA, 2015). We propose the correct question to be: what does the ideal end condition look like for us all? This slight semantic shift represents ideal societal end conditions as a holistic function of the various dual cosmos rather than a top-down value judgement, and repositions society's grand challenges as a balancing act between individual self-interest and optimal function of the systems of society in relation to their environments (people).We are, of course, not advocating for a new set of sustainable development goals (though they have already evolved from the initial millennium development goals adopted in 2000), but we are advocating for an examination of the SDGs through the lens of systemic type III errors to analyze the hesitancy to embracing the SDGs (UN DESA, 2021) and potentially overcome said hesitancy.

6.2 Social Entrepreneurship as a Tool for Systems Reflexivity: Learning from Type III Errors for Societal Change

"The type three error occurs when to *our* detriment *we unintentionally fool and trick ourselves* into solving the wrong problems precisely" (Mitroff & Silvers, 2010, p. 6). What might account for this unintentional distortion? In the pluralistic modern society, we fool and trick ourselves due to a fundamental misunderstanding of society and our places in it. A common interpretation of the social systems which govern modern society are premised on action theories following Giddens (1979), Bourdieu (1968), and Parsons (1951). The idea that actions introduce variation into the communication of meaning gives us a greater sense of control over the system. When grand challenges and SDGs are under discussion, we tend to think of them this way, as controlling the system. The very notion of grand challenges is how we might manufacture the systems of society to reach our ideal end conditions. This can and should be viewed as a type III error in itself. The notion that we have control over the systems of society, more than just influence, is a significant misrepresentation of the underlying problem: barriers to grand challenges, and wicked problems, are human problems not systems problems. Within the autopoietic society, the functional systems of the macrocosm (such as economic and political systems) are autopoietic self-referential processes which cannot be produced externally. That is, while human interaction may be a necessary condition for the emergence of these functional systems, humans cannot control them. The relation between humans and systems emerges through the system's internal process of self-organization which enables the system to respond to expected interactions with its environment (humans). In short, humans cannot change the system, but can encourage the system to change itself.

Humans can encourage the system to change itself by influencing its structures of reproduction. These self-organized structures mediate the interactions between humans and the system by allowing the system to adapt to perturbations form the environment. Thus, the role of humans is to manage the ways in which they perturb a system. For example, the economic system is a social system governing the payment of exchange. It reproduces based on binary communication codified as "pay/not pay". To maintain this reproduction through binary communications, the system generates a medium of exchange: money. As the economic system reproduces on the basis of its own payment logic, it begins to self-organize into structures as expectations of environmental (human) communication. These structures emerge against the backdrop of expected communications given various topics within the realm of exchange. For instance, the market is a structure of the economic system which has emerged in response to perturbations from the environment regarding the exchange of goods and services. Similarly, capitalism and communism emerged in response to perturbations from the environment regarding the social interactions incumbent in the exchange of goods and services. Humans did not create the market, nor did they create capitalism or communism. Rather, it would be more accurate to say that markets emerged as a structure of the economic system to enable it to respond to communications of "pay/no pay". Similarly, capitalism and communism emerged as structures of the economic system in response to the influence of private ownership in the payment of exchange.

Building on the above example, capitalism as a structure is a specific organization of the economic system whereby the system has adapted to the expected communications from the structures of its environment (humans). These human structures can be directly altered through the social interactions which have become interpenetrated to the system. Recalling that interpenetration refers to specific couplings of systems to the extent one (or both) systems treat each other like parts of their own, thus, our potential for influencing systems change begins with how we operate within existing structures. How we do that is a function of our ability to communicate extant shortcomings of system structures. As mentioned above, the type III error is fundamentally a communication problem. In fact, a type III error can only be observed, defined, and communicated by an individual or organization external to the individual or organization committing the type III error (Mitroff & Silvers, 2010). Furthermore, observation, definition, and communication of the type III error requires divergent cognitive responses from the committer of the type III error. In short, person A can only identify a type III error committed by person B if person A and person B have different conceptualizations of the given problem. Similarly, person B can only identify the type III error they've committed once it has been communicated to them. Only once this communication has taken place can person B learn from and then rectify an error of the third kind. Recalling Luhmann's theory of communication (utterance + information + understanding = communication) type III errors persist because rectifying an error of the third kind is a function of one's willingness (or ability) to process conflicting information from an external source.

6.3 Disruptive Communication in Practice: Examining some SDGs

Social entrepreneurship is a multi-level process of disruption which alters communication at each level of society. In so doing, the social entrepreneurship process implements innovative methods of altering one's willingness (or ability) to process conflicting information and learn from errors of the third kind. At the micro-level, social entrepreneurs communicate to external parties that the current relations between them and a given system are not enough. From this initial communicative disruption, they begin to disrupt the communications at the meso and macro level which often lead to type III errors and obfuscate positive societal change. Let's examine SDG 1 (no poverty), specifically 1.1 *By 2030, reduce at least by half the proportion of men, women and children of all ages living in poverty in all its dimensions according to national definitions* and 1.3 *Implement nationally appropriate social protection systems and measures for all, including floors, and by 2030 achieve substantial coverage of the poor and the vulnerable* (UNGA, 2015). Muhammad Yunus' Grameen Bank best illustrates the multi-tiered process of disrupting communications and learning from type III errors. Dr. Yunus and the Grameen Bank have successfully highlighted the shortcomings of traditional banking structures as organizations of the economic system, through a multi-level process of disrupting the communications between the economic, judicial, and psychic systems to pioneer the concepts of microcredit and microfinance. At the micro level, Dr. Yunus was spurred by the prevalence of loan sharking in the villages near the University of Chittagong, in Bangladesh. He began by going into the villages and talking to villagers about their situations, and was inundated with stories about entire families who lost everything because they borrowed small amounts of money and the lenders took everything from them on the basis of the loan conditions. Specifically, Sufiya Begum recounted to Dr Yunus:

> She relied on the local moneylender for the cash she needed to buy the bamboo for the stools she crafted. But he would only give her the money if she agreed to sell him all she produced, and at a price he would decide—which was ridiculously low. Thus, though hardworking, she was trapped in poverty. (Yunus et al., 2010. p. 314)

Conflicted by the inefficiencies of economic teachings (a discipline he taught!) for addressing the problem of loan sharking (Yunus, 2017), Dr Yunus decided to lend his own money to members of the village so they could avoid going to loan sharks. The choice to lend as an individual represents Dr Yunus' communication to villagers that their relation to the structures of the economic system through their informal institutions (in this case the norm of loansharking) were 'not enough'. Existing within these structures would keep them in a vicious cycle of poverty. Over time, he continued providing loans, villagers continued to pay him back, and he expanded his loans to other villages. This increase in demand led him to approach a bank to continue this work without running out of his own money. The banks repeatedly communicated that they could not support him because lending money to the poor wouldn't work—it couldn't work. Despite the evidence of individual repayments Dr Yunus received, banks still refused to consider poor people as viable customers (Yunus et al., 2010). In 1976, Dr Yunus attempted to create his own bank for the poor, which received further backlash—the formal institutions of the banking structure simply would not allow a bank for the poor, how could it? The traditional banking structure output loans based on collateral to ensure the economic system's logic of "pay/not pay". The poor could not provide collateral and thus you could not ensure repayment: the economic system simple could not translate (re) payment without collateral. In

1983, the Grameen Bank became a formal bank which operated in the villages and provided microcredits to the poor through credit rings to finance income generating activities (Yunus, 2007). These credit rings substituted the notion of traditional collateral by engaging villagers' social capital. That is, a credit ring is a group of five perspective borrowers who borrow as one. Only if the first two borrowers begin repaying will the others in the group become eligible for loans (Yunus et al., 2010). This ensured mutual management of repayment, thereby serving the same ends as collateral in the traditional banking system. At this point, the Grameen Bank operated at the meso level and reproduced on decisions regarding how to make the banking structures 'good enough' (in this case, the concept of credit rings). As the Grameen Bank continued its self-replication on these decisions, the economic system self-organized to recognize credit rings as a method of translating (re)payment without traditional capital, in villages.[4] The economic system's recognition of credit rings as a method of translating 'pay/not pay' has led to the Grameen Group: a model which has revolutionized the micro-finance industry and spread around the world.

Dr Yunus' efforts addressed type III errors at all three levels of society and, in doing so, acted as a reflexive lens which contributed to widespread poverty alleviation and a systemic pathway for the poor and the vulnerable to escape vicious cycles of poverty. At the micro level, Dr Yunus showed that borrowing from loansharks as a means of living one's lifestyle did not lift people out of poverty, despite being hard working and entrepreneurially competent, because borrowing from loansharks was an error of the III kind—while it allowed them to work it did not address the underlying problem of poverty. At the meso-level, Dr Yunus and the Grameen Bank showed that the 'problem' of collateral was the wrong problem to focus on because the absence of collateral did not adequately demonstrate a willingness to repay. Over time, repeatedly demonstrating the inadequacies of traditional collateral perturbed the economic system to the point it self-organized into a structure which recognized credit rings in terms of 'pay/not pay'. Here, Dr Yunus did not change the system, but created the conditions for the system to change itself.

The ideal end condition of no poverty is (relatively) straight forward. One could argue that addressing poverty involves a great deal of emphasis

[4] The Grameen bank does not operate in Bangladeshi cities and thus, the notion of traditional collateral is still a communicative mechanism whereby the economic system can process "pay/not pay"

on setting the conditions for the economic system to change itself in a way we might find ideal. So let's examine a grand challenge that is less straight forward. Take SDG 13 (climate action), as an example, specifically, 13.2: *Improve education, awareness-raising and human and institutional capacity on climate change mitigation, adaptation, impact reduction and early warning* (UNGA, 2015). In the first instance, improving education for meaningful behavior surrounding climate action requires the processing of information regarding what constitutes the wicked problem of dangerous human interference with the climate. This is the first challenge presented by pluralism. The People's Climate Vote, a survey of public opinion conducted by the United Nations Development Programme (UNDP), in partnership with Oxford University, found that 64% of people found climate change to be an emergency.[5] While that is well over half, there are still 36% who do not take this view of an emergency, signifying a discrepancy of over one-fifth of respondents who are less likely to inconvenience themselves in the name of climate action. In the second instance, education requires processing information which suggests that one's current style of living deviates from ideal conditions set forth by the United Nations Framework Convention on Climate Change (UNFCCC). That is, after accepting the danger of human interference with the climate, one must then accept that their individual behavior contributes to that interference (such as recycling vs. non recycling, biking vs. driving, or plant-based vs. meat-based diet). At this point, one must then accept that their individual behavior should be changed and must then accept plausible alternatives to their current behavior. In short, improving education and human capacity for motivating action on climate change requires the integration of 4 elements: (i) accepting that climate change is a condition of human activity, (ii) accepting that one's current lifestyle contributes to this climate change, (iii) accepting that they should change their lifestyle, and (iv) accepting plausible alternatives to current lifestyle.

The first of these three can be identified as normative: what should be done. The fourth represents a positive: what can be done. Pluralism emerges at all four of these steps. The first three we can assign to moral pluralism—why anyone should accept these three things are value judgements which cannot be empirically proven (Weber, 1985). Whether or not

[5] The People's Climate Vote had 1.2 million respondents spanning 50 countries covering the 56% of the world's population. The full climate vote report can be downloaded here: https://www.undp.org/publications/peoples-climate-vote

someone chooses to accept these elements and then act on them differs due to diverse (and rational) conceptualizations of what is good and desirable (Rawls, 1993). The fourth step is a function of an individual's context; what is plausible is determined by the context within which they find themselves, which we can summarize as the current relations between them and the social structures of their environment. For example, let's say that achieving the ideal conditions of SDG 13 requires less driving, more biking (or walking), less plastic usage, and a plant-based diet. Person A has accepted all 4 of the aforementioned elements and has made a conscious choice not to drive, not to own a car, recycle, and reduce meat consumption. Now let us assume that person A works 10km from home, opts to ride a bicycle to work, use less plastic, and eat less meat. Let us now assume Person B has the exact same conditions except that they have children they must drop off at school or daycare before work. In this instance, not owning a car becomes significantly less practical for person B than person A. While they both have accepted the normativity of actions that must be taken to work towards the ideal end conditions, from a practical perspective, person B has conflicting and rational moral imperatives towards their family which obfuscates their full engagement with SDG 13. To further add to the complexity, let's say that person B has less free time and disposable income due to having a larger family. In contrast to person A, let's assume person B uses their limited free time to purchase breakfast for themselves in between bringing children to school or daycare and arriving at work. For simplicity, person B opts to purchase a vegetarian wrap packaged in plastic. At the same time, they pack a relatively cheap meat-based school lunch (such as a ham and cheese sandwich) for their children wrapped in convenient single use packaging. Here, we see person B committing type III errors at the individual level as they seek to manage the complexities of their lives by opting for rational alternatives. While they have accepted the normative imperatives for changing their behavior, their practical realities have forced them to solve the real-life problems of their daily lives accurately (for example, buying meat-based lunch ingredients because it's cheaper or purchasing lunch wrapped in plastic because it's convenient).

In solving these problems, they further contribute to the climate crisis because they are addressing the 'wrong' (but arguably more pressing) problem. We contend that this decision to address the 'wrong' problem stems from existing communications between person B and the structures of their environment, specifically, the (incorrect) notion that a meat-based diet is cheaper and the market's incentivization for purchasing single use plastic as a means of cutting opportunity costs and enhancing convenience. In the thought experiment above, we see that cutting of opportunity cost (i.e. the loss of value incurred by engaging in an activity) and the convenience of plastic wrapping encouraged person B to act in ways that contributed to the wicked problem of dangerous human interference. Research has found that lower-middle income and low-income countries face an 18–29% cost increase when switching to a plant-based diet, but this increased cost shifts to an average of 37% cost decrease when accounting for reductions in food waste, which is important for the SDG 13 agenda (Springmann et al., 2021).[6] For person B to begin addressing the 'right' problem—human interference—without sacrificing their duty to family or work, the feasibility to address both must be communicated. In contrast to SDG 1, we can say that SDG 13 involves significantly more emphasis on the social system of 'social interaction' (Chap. 3) and how these social interactions relate to functional subsystems such as the economic system.

Social entrepreneurship communicates this middle ground at the micro level through innovative methods of articulating (Beckmann, 2011) the inefficient relations between individual people, social interactions, and the structures of their environment. Wilson, one of the participants of our netnographic studies, operates a social enterprise in the Netherlands which promotes vegan lifestyles and produce shopping as a means of moving towards SDG 13. He experiences significant challenges when trying to articulate the inefficiencies of the extant social structures for making meaningful lifestyle changes in the name of SDG 13:

> The biggest challenge is actually convincing people that the change that is required for them to shop with us is necessary. So it's an educational problem more than it is anything else. So it's the mental adjustment there is really big. It really is a different type of shopping. Also, it takes a bit longer. So it's slow shopping. You come into us, you take your time, so this kind of rushed running home from work to buy a pizza and throw it in the oven. It doesn't exist with us, we're a different type of shopping experience

To overcome this mental hurdle, Wilson engaged in the meso-level by partnering with local artisanal producers and further engaging with the

[6] The same study found that there was a cost decrease of up to 22–34% in upper-middle and high-income countries.

community through gardening events held at his shop. Including artisanal work in his shop provided beyond-vegan goods that might attract additional clients. During gardening events, various volunteers came forward to participate and discussed topics surrounding climate action. Particularly, the notion that one doesn't have to be a vegan to shop at a vegan store.

> We attracted a certain kind of person, and that kind of person wants to do good. They want to change their life for the better and they want to contribute to a better society but they don't know how. They're looking for answers as to how to make the world a better place. And we're just one little part of that. We're just a little shop that helps people feel better about themselves by changing their habits, by buying better and we've become part of a community of likeminded people

In Wilson's case, the disruptive communications (such as, you can shop here and not be a vegan) and community engagement (such as gardening events) may not be applicable to person B—remember, person B has already accepted the normativity of actions that must be taken to work towards the ideal end conditions. However, the social entrepreneurship process disrupts communications at the systems level through organizational self-replication based on decisions regarding how to make something 'good enough'. Wilson's social embeddedness sensitizes him to people in situations such as person B and he is moving towards helping people in such situations to avoid errors of the third kind that emerge from the balancing act of navigating existing structures:

> This year we're going to do online distribution by bicycle to our neighborhood. It's to deal with the convenience problem that we have because our shop is not a convenience store. It requires thinking, it requires planning. And it's not the kind of place where you can be walking home from work and you kind of just run in and pick something up for dinner. Well It is. But it requires a shift in one's thinking. But convenience is one of the biggest obstacles that we face in the business. So to deal with that convenience problem, we're going to do deliveries, but that raises the problem of packaging. So what we're going to do is we're gonna put everything in compostable packaging delivered to the neighborhood by bicycle, collect all the packaging along with the food waste of our customers and bring it back and actually compost it all ourselves out the back of the store. So we're actually creating a mini ecosystem based on selling food ingredients, people are cooking with it, we're taking back the food waste, we're taking back the packaging we sold it through and we're converting that into compost.

In Wilson's case, we can see how he is disrupting communication at each level of society to ameliorate and learn from type III errors as a means of changing social interactions to promote societal change. At the micro level, Wilson showed that the false narrative that a plant-based diet is more expensive is not the real problem because the affordability of the shop does not impact the mentality required to alter in-store shopping behavior. At the meso level, Wilson and his venture showed that emphasizing the first three elements mentioned above constitutes an error of the third kind because changing lifestyles for climate action is heavily determined by the convenience perceived in the practical alternatives as it relates to the structures of their environments. Over time, Wilson is repeatedly demonstrating the inadequacies of the current shopping structure with the hope of perturbing the social interactions within his local community to the point where the perceived convenience of vegan shopping promotes the lifestyle changes necessary to work towards SDG 13.

Returning to wicked problems and their relation to grand challenges, social entrepreneurship engages with open potential of solutions to wicked problems to continue moving iteratively closer to a "better than" solution until we achieve what might be determined as a correct solution. Indeed, recalling the propositions described in Chap. 1, wicked problems do not have an exhaustive set of potential solutions, and potential solutions to wicked problems are not true or false but rather described through words such as "better" or "worse". The communicative capacity embedded in the social entrepreneurship process and the involvement of the radical imaginary (i.e. making sense beyond what has already been made sense of), the social entrepreneurship process is vital as a testing bed for societal solutions to the wicked problems obfuscating grand challenges.

The aim of this book has been to suggest an alternative lens through which to rethink grand challenges and promote social entrepreneurship as a vital tool for achieving them. By introducing Luhmann's systems theory, we restructure the impetus for positive social change as a multi-level process of disrupting the communications which govern society, initiated by individual-level actors. This perspective highlights the ability of individuals to change the world by leveraging their experiences and communicative potential for disrupting the patterns of communication within a given context. Modern society is comprised of social interactions based on communications which influence the internal processes of the functional systems of society. As we seek to meet the grand challenges of our time, errors of the third kind emerge from the premise that barriers to achieving ideal end conditions are due to the faults of the system rather than the faults of social interaction.

The systems of society behave precisely as they are meant to as they continue their own reproduction. Grand challenges are human normative statements of the ideal conditions of these systems, whose achievement necessitates disrupting ongoing communications between people and the systems of society. We have demonstrated the human capacity to respond, adapt to, and navigate externally imposed disruption (such as COVID and environmental crises) and we have endeavored in this book to illustrate that achieving grand challenges requires internally disrupting communications between people as a means of encouraging systems to change themselves. Social entrepreneurship's embeddedness in the micro-level and the daily lives of the demographics it seeks to benefit presents a unique reflexive tool for disrupting communication which give life to type III errors. Positive societal change, however, cannot rely solely on social entrepreneurship. Decision-makers and practitioners at all levels should further incorporate individual persons in strategic planning through greater involvement of social entrepreneurship as a tool which captures, learns, adapts, and incorporates the complex pluralities of society. The plurality of views, opinions, and obligations of people living in the modern society invite multiple (and often conflicting) communications which guide how they interact with various systems in their daily lives. Only by disrupting these communications and recognizing the fundamental role of all individuals in the behavior of systems, can we effectively navigate the multiple disruptions of society and learn from the type III errors we commit and achieve the grand challenges of our time.

References

Adler, N. J., Freeman, R. E., & Quinn, R. E. (2016). Errors of the third kind in management research: Creating meaning in scholarly work. In *Academy of management proceedings* (Vol. 2016, No. 1, p. 10037). Academy of Management.

Ames, M. G. (2019). *The charisma machine: The life, death, and legacy of One Laptop per Child*. Mit Press.

Beckmann, M. (2011). The social case as a business case: Making sense of social entrepreneurship from an ordonomic perspective. In *Corporate citizenship and new governance* (pp. 91–115). Springer.

Bourdieu, P. (1968). Structuralism and theory of sociological knowledge. *Social Research, 35* (4), 681–706. Focus—Conservative Approaches in the Human Sciences.

Giddens, A. (1979). *Central problems in social theory: Action, structure, and contradiction in social analysis* (Vol. 241). University of California Press.

Kimball, A. W. (1957). Errors of the third kind in statistical consulting. *Journal of the American Statistical Association, 52*(278), 133–142.

Mitroff, I. I., & Featheringham, T. R. (1974). On systemic problem solving and the error of the third kind. *Behavioral Science, 19*(6), 383–393.

Mitroff, I. I., & Silvers, A. (2010). *Dirty rotten strategies: How we trick ourselves and others into solving the wrong problems precisely.* Stanford University Press.

Oliver, M. (2011). Technological determinism in educational technology research: Some alternative ways of thinking about the relationship between learning and technology. *Journal of Computer Assisted Learning, 27*(5), 373–384.

Onwuegbuzie, A. J., & Daniel, L. G. (2003). Typology of analytical and interpretational errors in quantitative and qualitative educational research. *Current issues in Education, 6*, 1–51.

Parsons, T. (1951). *The social system.* Psychology Press.

Piketty, T. (2014). *Capital in the 21st century.* President and Fellows, Harvard College.

Rawls, J. (1993). *Political liberalism.* Columbia University Press.

Raworth, K. (2017). *Doughnut economics: Seven ways to think like a 21st-century economist.* Chelsea Green Publishing.

Springmann, M., Clark, M. A., Rayner, M., Scarborough, P., & Webb, P. (2021). The global and regional costs of healthy and sustainable dietary patterns: A modelling study. *The Lancet Planetary Health, 5*(11), e797–e807.

United Nations General Assembly (UNGA). (2015). *Transforming our world: The 2030 agenda for sustainable development, resolution adopted by the general assembly on 25 September 2015.* A/RES/70/1 21 October 2015. New York: United Nations.

United Nations General Assembly (UNGA). (2021). *The sustainable development goals report 2021.* https://unstats.un.org/sdgs/report/2021/

Weber, M. (1985). *Gesammelte Aufsätze zur Wissenschaftslehre.* Hrsg. von Johannes Winckelmann. 6., erneut durchgesehene Auflage, Tübingen: J. C. B. Mohr (Paul Siebeck) (1. Auflage 1922)

Yunus, M. (2007). *Creating a world without poverty: Social business and the future of capitalism.* Public Affairs.

Yunus, M. (2017). *A world of three zeros: The new economics of zero poverty, zero unemployment, and zero net carbon emissions.* PublicAffairs.

Yunus, M., Moingeon, B., & Lehmann-Ortega, L. (2010). Building social business models: Lessons from the Grameen experience. *Long Range Planning, 43*(2–3), 308–325.

Index[1]

[1] Note: Page numbers followed by 'n' refer to notes.

E. Costales, A. Zeyen, *Social Entrepreneurship and Grand Challenges*, https://doi.org/10.1007/978-3-031-07450-9

The manufacturer's authorised representative in the EU is Springer Nature Customer Service Centre GmbH, Europaplatz 3, 69115 Heidelberg, Germany. If you have any concerns regarding our products, please contact ProductSafety@springernature.com

Printed and bound by CPI Group (UK) Ltd, Croydon, CR0 4YY
30/09/2026
02225475-0010